A P

THE G

Constantine Tsouc
born in Athens in 1937. He studied law, philosophy, and sociology in Athens, Heidelberg, Munich, Paris, and Yale. He practised law in Athens and did research at the Centre of Social Sciences there. Although his legal residence is still in Greece, he has lived abroad since December 1967 and is now living in Paris. At the moment he is collaborating with the French National Centre of Scientific Research (CNRS), and is lecturer in Political Sociology in the Experimental University Centre of Vincennes in Paris.

CONSTANTINE TSOUCALAS

The Greek Tragedy

PENGUIN BOOKS

Penguin Books Ltd, Harmondsworth, Middlesex, England
Penguin Books Inc., 7110 Ambassador Road, Baltimore, Maryland 21207, U.S.A.
Penguin Books Australia Ltd, Ringwood, Victoria, Australia

—

First published 1969

—

—

Made and printed in Great Britain
by C. Nicholls & Company Ltd
Set in Linotype Times

Contents

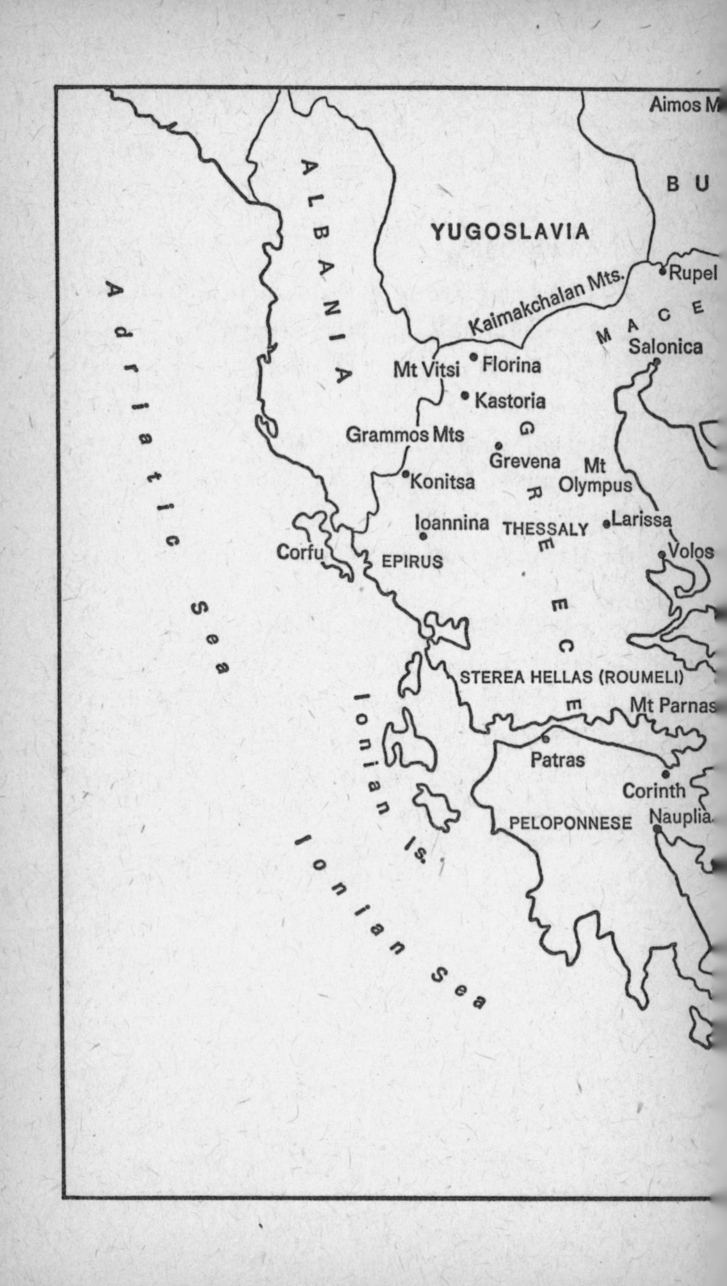
YUGOSLAVIA
ALBANIA
Aimos M
BU
Rupel
Kaimakchalan Mts.
MACE
Salonica
Mt Vitsi
Florina
Kastoria
Grammos Mts
Grevena
Mt Olympus
Konitsa
GREECE
Ioannina
THESSALY
Larissa
Volos
Corfu
EPIRUS
Adriatic Sea
STEREA HELLAS (ROUMELI)
Mt Parnas
Ionian Is.
Patras
Corinth
Nauplia
PELOPONNESE
Ionian Sea

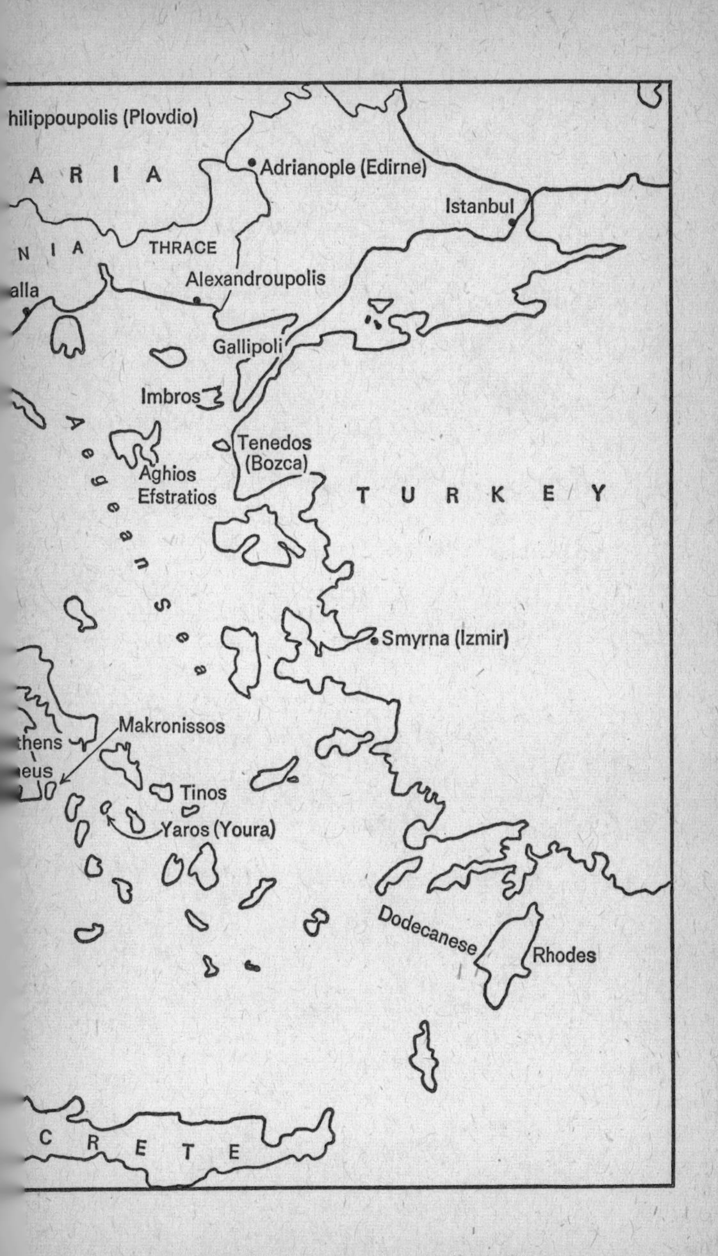
hilippoupolis (Plovdio)
A R I A
Adrianople (Edirne)
Istanbul
N I A
THRACE
Alexandroupolis
alla
Gallipoli
Imbros
Aegean Sea
Tenedos (Bozca)
Aghios Efstratios
T U R K E Y
Smyrna (Izmir)
Makronissos
thens
eus
Tinos
Yaros (Youra)
Dodecanese
Rhodes
C R E T E

Introduction

DICTATORSHIPS do not come out of the blue. The military *coup* of 21 April 1967 may indeed have come as a shock to international opinion. But for the Greek people military dictatorship had for long been a conceivable, even probable, turn of events. The object of this book is to provide an explanation of the origins of these events and of the constellation of social, political and international forces which made them possible.

An adequate understanding of the forces currently at work in Greece requires considerable probing into their sources and historical evolution. Yet this book is not meant as a historical narrative. The aim is not to tell the story but to provide a framework for its interpretation. Hence the treatment of periods and subjects is not uniform. Emphasis is rather directed to a few highly selected recent periods when intense socio-political activity produced important shifts which modified the underlying structure. The new trends thus set provide in turn an explanation for the system's further evolution. At each major turning point special attention must be given to the interrelation between domestic Greek forces and the influence of the dominant international power blocs. More so than in the case of other countries, this interplay of national and international factors is of paramount importance for understanding modern Greece.

The formation of modern Greece in the nineteenth century is a necessary starting-point. The creation of the modern 'bourgeois' Greek state after the Balkan Wars of 1912–13 and the achievements of the Liberal Party and its foreign policy, particularly directed to the consolidation of the strong tie with Britain, set the stage for the eventual struggle between Right and Left and for the process of international involvement. The narrative then focuses on the major events resulting from the Second World War: occupation, resistance, civil war. For it is the turmoil of the 1944–9 period which substantially explains present Greek realities. The defeat of the Left, first in 1944 and then again in 1949, did not merely result in the maintenance of the capitalist system in Greece. More fundamentally, those defeats determined the forms which the post-war regime was to take, its ideological and cultural orientations, its critical dependance on foreign centres of power and therefore also the modes of its internal evolution. It is in fact with a striking degree of directness that the outcome of the civil war of twenty years before led to the 1967 *coup* and to the regime of the colonels who have been in power since. Most of the book is concerned with tracing the chain from the one upheaval to the other.

The colonels' regime as such is not, however, analysed. The lack of serious information on the development of socio-political forces under the dictatorship would make any attempt to cover the subject fallacious. A different type of analysis, or straightforward polemical writing, is of course possible. Journalists have exposed the police measures, the tortures, the naïve populism and the contradictory social and economic policies of the regime. The resistance organizations inside Greece and Greek parliamentarians in exile have analysed the present situation and put forward their programmes. Numerous European governments have openly condemned the regime and its policies, and Mr Harold Wilson has used the word 'bestialities' to describe them. The information on which these attacks are based its plentiful – but it is not adequate for a more analytical view of how the dictatorship functions as a socio-political system. We simply do not know enough about the internal evolution of the junta in power, about the existence or significance of contradictory trends within it, and about the *precise* role of foreign powers, particularly of the United States. For all that is at present known, leaked or simply rumoured, it may be that the only operational centre of 'Greek' politics is actually in Washington, D.C., or in its outskirts.

Some problems can, however, be anticipated. The events of recent years, particularly since the fraudulent elections organized under Karamanlis in 1961, have shown that Greece was becoming ripe for a European-type progressive movement. The wounds of civil war had been healed; the traditional Right had shrunk decisively and was on the way to becoming a permanent minority. Domestic political forces had evolved outside the straitjacket of post-war years: strong governing Right, meek decorative Centre, and (by definition) 'dangerous' Left. In due course, a modern social-democratic party was bound to evolve. There was already talk of the Centre-Left, even of a New Left. Thus the signs were read. And the *coup* was a proof that the trend towards political democracy and social modernization was interpreted correctly – by all sides.

The existence of dictatorship is, of course, not by itself enough to nullify the forces just cited. But it can certainly contain them for a long time. The new regime is a manifestation of a technical possibility inherent in all modern societies, by virtue of an enormously increased and perfected system of coercion. A modern, internationally protected totalitarian movement of fascist inspiration (whatever name it might find desirable in given circumstances) does not necessarily need what its pre-war counterparts depended on to conquer and hold power – namely, a large and politically conscious popular base organized into a party. The mere inertia of the mass of the population, be it of skilful manipulation or of repression or of both, might suffice to keep a small clique in power, so long as it controls a determined body holding the material means of coercion. Thus, the repeated assertion by the dictators that democracy will be restored when the Greek people are 'ripe' for it probably means: 'We look forward to the time when the people are persuaded or manipulated into not caring any more.' Meanwhile, an elaborate repressive arsenal can reasonably hope to keep under control any expression of discontent, provided that this does not reach the level of a massive popular outburst.

This last possibility must not, however, be excluded. It is naturally more unlikely until widely felt economic dissatisfaction is added to the general atmosphere of political suffocation under the dictatorship. The economic recession which has replaced the boom of the years before the *coup* does seem to have developed into permanent stagnation even though the colonels or their advisers can read Keynes. A major crisis has so far been avoided and can probably be avoided for some time. The economic situation is however likely to remain extremely critical.

A number of measures taken by the colonels clearly indicate that they are seriously trying to build a permanent power structure. The control of all trade unions, syndicates and collective bodies from above; the newly defined role of the religious authorities as makers of ideology; the appointment of government 'commissioners' in public organizations and private corporations alike; the decision-making role allocated to 'representatives of the producing classes', naturally appointed by the government – all this recalls the corporate state of Mussolini and Salazar.

Perhaps more to the point, the new 'constitutional' definition of the armed forces as a body placed above and beyond the political sphere, and their enhanced status as guarantors of the regime, shows that those who have seized power by the sword intend to go on living by it. Yet, if the institutional framework is more or less apparent, there is only sparse knowledge of how the newly integrated elements of the political system really function. And inevitably, the more obscure the actual political decision-making is, the more mystifying and myth-loaded are the institutional changes. If the intentions of the country's new rulers are manifest, their true position within their own system is unknown.

Thus, the question of whether a clash between the wishes of the people and the power of the rulers can be averted is still open. The outcome remains in the balance so long as the battle is not fully joined, either inside Greece or internationally. At the moment, however, the potential of active opposition by the Greek people, although developing, still remains a potential. The demonstrations by half a million people at George Papandreou's funeral showed that the farcical plebiscite organized by the colonels in September 1968 was simply rigged. However, we are still ignorant about the effects of the disruption of normal political life on the mass of the population, especially the peasants. Even at the risk of seeming pessimistic, it must at present be said that the forces which will shape the future of Greece are still unknown.

However, the matter does not stop here. Despite the lack of specific information, one fact is abundantly clear. The regime still lacks a stable base of domestic support which could enable it to function freely, and has not even secured the massive apathy, or the frustration of its potential enemies, which could insure it against attacks from 'below'. Hence the need for permanent repression in all fields of activity. Hence also its chronic dependence on foreign – which means American – support. The last element, while providing the regime with its 'daily bread', contains the seeds of danger and uncertainty. You only receive unqualified support while you are necessary to the supporters. In the present explosive Middle Eastern situation, Papadopoulos's threat of '*après moi le déluge*' is probably incisive to military if not political ears. But international life is subject to change and a time may come when the lack of a strong domestic basis would seriously impair the international bargaining power of the regime. The standards of modern imperialism are not rigidly economic.

The new government has in fact offered unprecedented advantages to foreign capital (which, incidentally, has not for the time being manifested any great eagerness). But Greece is so restricted a market and so poor a source of raw materials that, however welcome (on both sides) foreign economic domination might be, the decisive factors must be political and strategic. And these might be modified even in the USA. It is in this context that the attitude of the Greek people is a factor of critical importance. An organized and coherent opposition against a government which can claim only the possession of the brute means of power provides a strong horse for outsiders to place a bet on. It reduces the negotiating power of the regime to nil. It might even, given the circumstances, precipitate an international interest to terminate the 'protection' from which the colonels depend for their current subsistence.

Thus, once again, two apparently contradictory maxims

seem to be in operation: that the fate of the Greek people rests in their own hands; and that Greece is always governed in whichever way the dominant international power sees fit. In the long run, it must be the former maxim that will carry more weight. But at what cost? The latter may have the advantage of flexibility and rapidity.

At the level of international politics, a new factor may turn out to be pivotal in the near future. This is the role of Western European countries. Greece has been an international problem before. But perhaps for the first time it now is a specifically European problem as well. In so far as the Europeans decide to pull their full weight, the painful experience of a single power having decisive influence over Greek affairs may be open to amendment.

*

I am indebted to so many people in writing this short book that I cannot hope to mention them all. I would like however specially to thank George Krimpas, who went through the whole manuscript with me. Many strenuous mistakes and omissions were corrected thanks to his efforts and his contribution to the final shaping of the book has been invaluable. I also want to express my profound gratitude to Mervyn Jones, who adapted the text stylistically with painstaking care.

C.T.

Paris, March 1969

CHAPTER 1

The Emergence of Independent Greece (1821–1909)

In almost a century and a half of modern Greek history, foreign intervention or foreign support has almost always been responsible – to a greater or lesser extent – for the birth and outcome of every crisis. Domestic social and political forces have never been able to develop or function autonomously. The Greek people have thus been powerless to take their destinies into their own hands: most flagrantly so when there was the most to win or lose. For, whatever the strategic and diplomatic line-up, Greece could not escape international attention because of her geographical situation. As a pawn of Western diplomacy when the Ottoman Empire was breaking up, as a naval base essential for the control of the Dardanelles, as a bastion of the 'Free World' in its attempt to stop the expansion of Communism, or as one of the very few secure bases for the strategic control of the ever-unstable Middle East, Greece has always had to pay the price for the international interest she has provoked.

To capture the essence of this continuous interaction between internal evolution and foreign intervention, we must survey the development of Greece that contains the origins of the present.

It is difficult to pin down the historical and cultural character of the Greek nation – Balkan but not Slav, Near Eastern but not Moslem, European but not Western. It may or may not be possible to trace a racial, cultural and national continuity from the classical period through the Byzantine Empire to modern Greece; the undoubted fact is that the origins of the modern social and economic structure are deeply rooted in the long period of Ottoman rule.

The Byzantine Empire was never a national state. If the Hellenic element was culturally preponderant, especially in the later period, the Empire was always a formless conglomeration of nationalities, united under the authority of the Imperial Orthodox state, the continuation and culmination of the Eastern Roman Empire. Only in the twelfth century, after signs of impending disintegration had become manifest, and especially when Ottoman power had thrown the Empire into eclipse, did the Greeks acquire a definite consciousness of national identity distinguishing them from the other ethnic groups of the Balkan peninsula and Anatolia. This sharp national consciousness contrasted with the lack of physical separation between Greeks and other groups, for the ever-changing geographical distribution of the various Balkan nationalities was far from homogeneous. Except for the islands and the southern part of the peninsula, where the population was mainly Greek, and for the regions north of the Aimos mountains, where the Slav element was dominant, the great bulk of the Balkans was inhabited by a heterogeneous mixture of Greeks, Serbs, Bulgarians, Wallachians, Rumanians, Albanians and of course Turks – the Greek element being more concentrated in the towns and along the coasts, and the Slavs becoming more numerous in the mountains and plains of the interior. Greek predominance was greatest in Constantinople and the few large commercial and cultural centres of the Ottoman Empire: Salonica, Ioannina, Adrianople, Philippoupolis, Iassi, Smyrna, Alexandria. The Ottoman ideology, with its rigid social divisions, maintained a disdainful attitude to mercantile activities; this enabled the Greeks, and to a lesser degree other minority groups like the Jews and the Armenians, virtually to monopolize business life. The Greek community of Constantinople, consisting of the remnants of the Byzantine aristocracy and of the emerging groups of bankers and merchants known as Phanariots, rapidly gained control of the greater part of economic transactions. The role of the Phanariots, however, was not confined to the financial sphere. They were often called upon to play a significant political and administrative part in the Ottoman power system – both in the capital, where they soon rose to extremely prominent positions, and in the provinces, where they were often entrusted with governmental functions, sometimes even on a hereditary basis.

The Greek element was also predominant in the commercial, entrepreneurial and maritime activities which grew rapidly after the middle of the eighteenth century, and infused a new spirit into the lethargic life of the Balkans. The prestige of this nascent Greek bourgeoisie, through which the new revolutionary ideas fermenting in Europe, especially after 1789, were chan- elled into the Balkans, became gradually paramount among both Greek and Slav peoples. The idea of a movement for independence, leading to an All-Balkan federation, was spreading, mainly under the instigation of Russia, while the widespread decay of the Ottoman Empire roused strong hopes of approaching independence in all social classes throughout the Balkan peninsula.

This process culminated in the Greek revolution of 1821. But, after considerable successes in the first years of the struggle, the reorganized Turkish–Egyptian army managed to win decisive victories which led to a political stalemate. By 1827 the revolution – which had been restricted to the Aegean islands, the Peloponnese and the southern part of the main peninsula (Sterea Hellas) – was nearly expiring.

It was then that the intervention of the foreign powers became decisive. The atrocities committed during the war and the romantic aura of the Hellenic past had greatly excited international public opinion. Popular pressure and diplomatic interests converged for once, and the great powers decided to take the situation in hand. Russia, France and Great Britain destroyed the Turkish–Egyptian fleet at Navarino (1827) and thus secured Greek independence.

To see how important these powers were in ensuing events, we must look briefly at the policies which they pursued. Russian policy was based on the idea of creating a large Balkan Greco–Slav state under her protection, to ensure her a stronghold in the Mediterranean after the breakdown of Ottoman power. Most of the population of the Balkans was Slav, and all subscribed to the Christian Orthodox faith; these were the two main propaganda instruments serving Russian aims. By contrast, British policy was basically oriented towards the conservation of the Ottoman Empire, as a counterbalancing power against Russian expansionism. To the extent, however, that the growing centrifugal forces within the Empire made its disintegration unavoidable in the long run, Great Britain favoured the creation of an independent Greek state which would, however, be politically and economically dependent on Britain, and therefore openly antagonistic to the other ethnic groups in the Balkans. The Protocol of London (1830), through which Greek independence was finally recognized, was a victory for British policy. The decision to install an absolute monarchy was aimed at the replacement of the first Greek Governor, Ioannis Kapodistrias, an ex-minister of the Tsar and naturally inclined towards Russian conceptions. Meanwhile, the restriction of the independent state's boundaries to a very small area, inhabited by a comparatively homogeneous population, made the new-born State absolutely dependent on foreign (that is British) economic and diplomatic support, and eventually led to antagonism between Greeks and Slavs. Thus, for more than a century, the Balkan peninsula was to be the most turbulent spot in Europe and the scene of continual struggles between interventionist powers. The idea of a federation uniting the Christian peoples of the European provinces of the Ottoman Empire, who had been living in relative harmony with one another for four centuries, was shelved. Britain, Russia, France, Austria and later Germany fought over the future of these provinces; their peoples paid and are still paying the bill.

After independence, the social and economic structure of Greece remained basically unchanged. The semi-feudal system prevailing under the Ottoman regime disappeared; but the land owned by Turkish feudal lords, amounting to about half the cultivated area of the country, passed in the main into the hands of the local chiefs and notables. These chieftains had played a significant role during the Ottoman period. They had been entrusted with considerable administrative and representational powers, especially in those villages which had been granted a certain degree of autonomy. After an ambiguous attitude in the first months of the War of Independence, they joined the revolutionary movement and played an important role. Very soon, however, they were involved in bitter struggles with the popular elements, which sometimes led to brutal armed conflicts. The outcome of class antagonism between local chieftains and popular forces was still inconclusive when independence was proclaimed. Under pressure from the chieftains, Kapodistrias hesitated to distribute the land among the impoverished peasants. When Kapodistrias was murdered by members of one of the most powerful clans, and when King Otto Wittelsbach, second son of King Ludwig I of Bavaria, was placed on the throne, the antiquated social structure was safeguarded. It was to take almost a century to achieve the necessary reforms and solve the land problem.

This, then, is Greece in 1832: a small country, utterly devastated after a terrible war lasting almost ten years, with a 95 per cent peasant population and an archaic, semi-feudal structure. The new state is not even the centre of Hellenism. No city of any importance is included within its boundaries. Its cultural, religious and economic centres are all abroad. Out of a total of three million Greeks, barely 700,000 are living in the Greek state. When Athens became the second capital of the country (after Nauplia) it was a miserable village with no more than 5,000 inhabitants – hardly to be compared with Constantinople, the symbol of national and religious regeneration, seat of the Patriarchate, centre of the Phanariots and the Greek bourgeoisie, swarming with Greek schools and publishing houses, housing the 'Great School of the Nation', a university of high prestige, and with a Greek population of over 200,000.

Naturally, the new state's main preoccupation was to try to liberate those Greek-inhabited regions that were still under Turkish rule. But although this natural urge towards national fulfilment was of supreme importance to Greeks, and although in itself it did not directly conflict with the interests of the other Balkan nationalities, it quickly degenerated into a utopian dream of rebuilding the Byzantine Empire under Greek sovereignty. The 'Great Idea', as this conception came to be called, was the main ideological and political slogan throughout the century. The repercussions of this orientation are enormous, both in domestic and in foreign policy. The solution of all internal problems was usually shelved by means of skilful demagogy, in the name of the national unity necessary to make the dream come true. Time after time the realization of this dream is successfully called upon to divert public attention from the incapacity or unwillingness of the ruling groups to take the measures required by the permanently frustrating internal situation. It is true that the glorification of 'Hellenic' values, which constitutes the cultural parallel to the 'Great Idea', did much to develop national unity and consciousness. The mystifying power of the notions of 'Eternal Greece' and 'cultural unity of the Greek people', however, resulted in serious ideological distortions which have yet to be completely dissipated. For not only did the mystical orientation towards classical antiquity constitute a major obstacle to a realistic and progressive national outlook; it also led to the imposition of a 'pure' language, reintroducing grammatical elements of ancient Greek, completely strange to the spoken idiom and to a certain extent incomprehensible to the common people. The contradiction between official and spoken language dominated the second half of the century and became the main cultural issue. The educational obscurantism which persists up to the present day is to a large extent due to the fact that conservative political forces have managed to identify the 'purity' of the language, symbol of the eternity of the nation, with the conservation of retrograde and mystifying educational and cultural values.

The international repercussions of the 'Great Idea' were even more far-reaching. Uncontrolled and intransigent nationalism led to chauvinism and pushed the country into conflict with the similarly motivated neighbouring Balkan countries, a conflict which haunts Balkan relations to the present day. Imperialist antagonism between the powers, and especially between Britain and Russia, did much to aggravate the problem. Throughout the nineteenth century the powers continued to instigate or to repress the outbursts of their diplomacy, and not hesitating to use direct military intervention. When, at the outbreak of the Crimean War (1853), Russia induced Greece to support revolutionary movements in Thessaly and Macedonia, the Anglo-French answer was prompt. French and British troops landed at the port of Piraeus and Greece was virtually occupied for three years (1854–7). After the departure of the troops, the country was formally declared to be under economic control by the powers.

Meanwhile, the evolution of the socio-economic structures of the country was extremely slow. The absolute monarchy of King Otto, surrounded by a large Bavarian court, was characterized by total disregard of the real needs and aspirations of the Greeks. Both the common people, who lived in a state of absolute misery, and the leading strata, who had emerged during and after the revolution (landowners, notables and military leaders), were intensely dissatisfied. The Bavarian administration had installed an undisguised despotism and ruled in complete separation from the indigenous forces. This state of affairs was only slightly modified by the revolution of 1844, which resulted in the promulgation of the first Greek Constitution. The limitations imposed on the monarch's absolute powers were nominal, and therefore the machinations of the three major parties openly representing the interests of the foreign 'protectors' (characteristically named the English, French and Russian parties respectively) were openly and unequivocally directed towards acquiring the royal favour.

It is only after the ending of economic control in 1860 that some progress is visible. A new political generation emerged and the first signs of early capitalist development were manifest. If industrial activity was still extremely limited, the boom in the merchant navy, tripled since 1838, and the spectacular growth of commerce resulted in the creation of a rising bourgeoisie. Though the main centres of economic and cultural activity were still abroad, the prestige of the national state was growing. A considerable amount of Greek-owned capital was invested in the country and began to constitute a strong pole of attraction for Greeks abroad. This trend gathered pace among the Greek bourgeoisie of Constantinople and the other large cities of the Ottoman Empire, for they lived under the threat of hostility from the Ottoman government. Though the

Sultan was forced to sign a series of proclamations protecting the rights of non-Moslem inhabitants, these fears were reinforced by the permanent state of cold or hot war (there were frequent outbursts of liberation movements) which marked Greco–Ottoman relations throughout the century.

The Bavarians were generally hated, and the emerging political forces were backed by Britain, suspicious of Otto's vacillating foreign policy. He was dethroned in 1862. The new king was Prince George Glücksburg of Denmark. The change marked a definite shift of Greek policy from the Russian to the British orbit. As a gesture of friendship, the British-occupied Ionian islands were handed to Greece in 1864. As the decaying Ottoman Empire grew unable to resist the impact of internal and external pressures, Britain based her policy on strengthening Greece against her Slav neighbours. Whenever the Balkan peoples tended to unite against the Sultan, Britain imposed a veto, for she was still haunted by the nightmare of a Balkan federation under Russian influence. In 1867 the Greek Prime Minister signed a treaty with Serbia, Rumania and Montenegro declaring that the future of the Balkans should be considered an internal Balkan affair; the British put pressure on King George and the government was immediately dismissed. Again, on the eve of the Russo–Turkish war in 1877, Greece was forced by Britain to turn down Serbian proposals for a common offensive against Turkey. When, however, at the end of the war, the treaty of San Stefano strengthened the Slav states to a considerable extent at the expense of Greece, not only did the British insist on a revision of the treaty and finally obtain a considerable curtailment of the Slav territorial gains through the treaty of Berlin (1878), but moreover, during subsequent negotiations with Turkey, they insisted on the cession of Thessaly and a part of Epirus to Greece (1881). Thus, not only was the territorial balance successfully maintained against Russia; Britain also postponed an eventual Balkan coalition through the intensification of inter-Balkan grievances resulting from the treaties.

The period after 1864, when the first democratic Constitution was promulgated, and especially from 1875 to 1895, was characterized by the first major effort to modernize the economic and administrative structure. Charilaos Trikoupis dominated the period with his outstanding personality and held power, with minor interruptions, for twenty years. His great achievement was an unprecedently ambitious programme of public works. Road mileage was multiplied tenfold between 1863 and 1909, the foundations of a modern railway network were laid, a series of ports suitable for large steamships were constructed, and the Corinth Canal was opened. The civil service, Army and Navy were completely reorganized. The results of this thorough modernization of the infrastructure were rapidly felt. The merchant fleet reached a total of 400,000 tons by 1895, commerce flourished, and several large banks opened their doors and created the basis for a modern credit system. The country entered a phase of rapid overall economic development. Industrial production also made progress: industrial potential, measured in horsepower, was twenty times greater in 1889 than in 1867.

However, Greece was still far from being an industrialized country. Despite spectacular growth, development had a commercial and financial emphasis. The urban proletariat was still rudimentary; only at the turn of the century did the number of industrial workers reach 20,000. Though a trade union movement began very early and many strikes were organized, the unions were still too weak, small and scattered for their political and social effect to be more than marginal. The class that emerged strongly in this period was the small bourgeoisie. The urban population rose from 8 per cent in 1853 to 28 per cent in 1879. These new city-dwellers constituted the big change in the social structure during the later nineteenth century.

Inevitably, the political structure of Greece was affected by the rise of the middle class. It was the natural social basis for growing liberal forces, of which Trikoupis was the outstanding representative. Both the industrial and the financial bourgeoisie backed the liberal movement, while conservatism was based on the old ruling class of large landowners. They owned 75 per cent of the cultivated land – in a century that was still predominantly agrarian – and their main concern was to prevent the impending land reform. The landless peasants, because of their extreme backwardness and lack of education, could not organize themselves as a significant political force, although a number of peasant revolts took place in the 1880s and were violently suppressed. On the whole, the peasants remained under the influence of the landlords and local notables. Only toward the end of the century did the demand for land reform become so widespread as to be a political factor of national importance.

Faced with opposition, Trikoupis hesitated to put through land reform. Here he made a grave mistake. For not only did this prolong the underdevelopment of Greek agriculture; it also permitted the survival of the landowners as a separate powerful class, which eventually resulted in the failure of the liberal movement and his government's downfall.

The most important failure of Trikoupis, however, occurred in financial policy. The great increase in public expenditure due to the multiplication of public works was not covered by reorganization of the taxation system, which remained organized on a feudal basis. Taxes were mainly indirect and extremely inegalitarian, except for a poll-tax, a remnant of the feudal Turkish system. There was no property or income tax. Revenue, although increasing, was not able to cover public expenses. Trikoupis therefore turned to borrowing from domestic and foreign capital. But the large, mainly British, loans which he obtained from abroad only aggravated the situation. For not only were the loans provided at a considerable discount from nominal value; they were only given when guaranteed by the cession of important branches of the state revenues. This led to the point where repayment of the foreign debt consumed more than 40 per cent of the government's revenues. Increasing economic dependence naturally led to stronger political dependence. Even if he had desired it, Trikoupis could not have possibly escaped from the clutches of British protection.

The dependence on domestic capital, which financed the public expenses to an equal degree, proved to be even more deadly to the liberal government. Private Greek capital controlled more and more of the state's sources of revenue. Thus the financiers flourished on the difficulties of the liberal state which they were themselves trying to build on the political level. Unwilling to transform their banking and commercial mentality, the ascending financial world defeated its own purposes. While the domestic capital interests of the time refused to take the risks of contributing to the effective industrial and economic development of the country, they demanded the fulfilment of the state's legal obligations to the letter. The effect of the combined external and internal pressures was that Trikoupis was obliged to declare a state of national bankruptcy (1893). Two years later, he was out of power.

The fall of Trikoupis, who, like many other Greek statesmen, was to die in self-imposed exile, marks the failure of the first serious attempt by the Greek liberal bourgeoisie to take over and create a modern state. The social strata that had helped the liberals to come to power retreated to at least temporary conservatism. The workers, and even more so the peasants, suffered severely from the regular increases in taxation imposed to cope with growing financial difficulties. Meanwhile, the hesitancy manifested towards the problem of land redistribution prevented the creation of a new class of support for the liberal policies. Through the loss of its natural allies, the progressive Greek bourgeoisie lost the support necessary to confront successfully the traditional political establishment of vested landed interests.

The conservatives thus returned to power after the fall of Trikoupis. The period from 1895 to 1907 saw a substantial setback in Greece's economic development. Foreign trade fell in volume and domestic commercial activity declined. The new government could not solve the problem of the external debt, and a state of permanent depression set in. Faced with rising popular discontent, the government had recourse to the 'Great Idea'. Public opinion was aroused; in 1897, despite economic depression and a total lack of military preparations, the government was pushed into declaring war on Turkey. It took only a few weeks for the Turkish Army, reorganized under the direction of German officers, to crush the disorganized and demoralized Greek Army under Crown Prince Constantine and to invade Greek territory, meeting virtually no resistance.

It was only because of strong international – mainly British – pressure that Greece suffered no more than insignificant territorial losses. German influence in the Ottoman Empire, growing since the Treaty of Berlin in 1878, had produced new anxieties for Britain. Since the final dismemberment of Ottoman power could not be far off, a weakening of Greece, the only stable representative of British interests in the Balkans, could be fatal. The key question was that of the future of Macedonia, the heart and military centre of the peninsula, and the scene of an intense diplomatic, propaganda and military struggle between all the Balkan nationalities, each putting forward historical, demographic and diplomatic arguments to claim the whole area for themselves.

But if the defeat had no territorial results, its moral impact was enormous. Known to everyone as 'the shame of 1897', it was the turning-point which led to the abandonment of the 'Great Idea' in its pure form. In view of the glaring contradiction between the conservative government's professed aim of rebuilding 'historic Hellas' and the incapacity and weakness of the Greek state, it was understood on all sides that profound structural reforms were needed before another military venture could be made. Discontent was deepest in the ranks of the Army. Junior officers in particular held the political world in general to blame for the frustration of all national aspirations. The monarchy too was called into question, for the King and his sons were held responsible for the incompetence and demoralization of the Army command.

Weak governments, formed by unstable coalitions, preserved a precarious balance for the decade after the defeat. But anti-Royalist feeling in the Army was intensified by the government's attitude in the crisis of 1905, when Cretan national forces led by Eleftherios Venizelos rebelled against the policy of Prince George of Greece, then Governor of Crete and totally subservient to British interests. Under the impact of liberal ideas which were again in ascendancy, the growing dissatisfaction in the Army took the form of a secret society, under the name of the 'Military League', mainly made up of junior officers of bourgeois origin. In cooperation with a group of young radical politicians, this group presented an ultimatum demanding the immediate reorganization of the Army, a new constitution limiting the power of the King to intervene in politics, the ousting of the royal family from the Army command and a radical purge of the administrative apparatus.

The ultimatum was rejected and the Union of Officers proclaimed a revolution (1909).

The revolution of 1909 marks the end of an era. As we shall see, the bourgeois ascendancy is thereby consolidated. The last remnants of feudalism will be dissipated. Greece is entering a new phase.

CHAPTER 2

The Creation of the Bourgeois State (1909–22)

THE military revolt of 1909 did not have an explicit ideological and political content. It was the culmination of a long process of discontent and exasperation against the leading political factions and the Palace. Its demands were founded on the nationalist aspirations of the young officers, which seemed irrevocably nullified by the incompetence and selfishness of the governing oligarchy. Yet the military ultimatum of Colonel Zorbas achieved much more than it had aimed for. Backed by the overwhelming majority of the middle classes, who found in the revolution a sudden chance for a radical modification of the system, the military revolutionaries discovered that they had not only imposed their moderate demands, but had in reality become the only organized power in the country. King George I, with considerable political foresight, did not try to intervene and the political oligarchy of the clans, which had ruled over Greece for almost a century, found itself denuded of all authority.

Their control over the country had been based on the monopoly they exercised over the political parties. Growing unrest since 1900 had already given birth to a number of progressive and socialist-oriented movements. But whereas these movements were still in their infancy, the military revolution had served as a catalyst for the virtually universal opposition which had been ready to explode, but had up to then failed through lack of an inspired leadership.

That this underlying class antagonism between the ruling caste and the ascending bourgeoisie had not previously taken open and defined political forms can be partly explained by the fact that there was no formal feudal system in Greece and thus divergencies in interests were much less rigidly defined than they had been in Western Europe. Hence the Trikoupis experiment had proved to be premature. But by 1909 the situation had changed radically. The middle classes had been further strengthened, especially under the impetus of the booming merchant navy[1] and the rapid development of the banking system; the example of the Young Turks' revolution which had overthrown the Sultan only a year ago had revived the hopes of the radicals; and the economic policy of the successive governments had become more and more oppressive for both the middle classes and the peasants. The successive tax increases on essential goods put the main burden on the workers and the middle classes, who had by now begun to organize in commercial guilds and unions. In March 1909 thousands of shopkeepers had violently demonstrated, in Athens and Piraeus, against the unequally distributed taxation. On 14 September a huge rally of over 50,000 (out of a population of under 200,000) shook Athens. While declaring their full confidence in the 'revolution', the Athenians went beyond the officer's intentions. The demands for a system of progressive income taxation, the protection of production, the transformation of the civil service into a body of true public servants by the abolition of the spoils system rampant till then, an improvement in the workers' standard of living, and a ban on usury as a criminal offence expressed the class antagonism that had been politically silent for so long. At the same time, the organization of the workers had been strengthened by the creation of numerous trade unions, and the discontent among the peasants had been growing since 1898, when the crisis in the currant trade, which had constituted a staple export, had reduced large strata of the agrarian population to misery. Unrest was especially strong in Thessaly, where the demand for agrarian reform of the large 'estate-system', inherited from the Turks, led to a series of violent peasant revolts, between 1905 and 1910, which had been bloodily repressed.

Thus when the Military League entrusted the political leadership of the new movement to Eleftherios Venizelos, a young Cretan lawyer who had distinguished himself during the

1. Greek tonnage rose from 8,241 in 1875 to 893,650 in 1915.

wars for independence of his home island, the Greek bourgeoisie found itself in power so suddenly that there was no established political formation to take advantage of the situation. This proved to be all to the good. Venizelos, who had been called in precisely to fill the political gap, was quickly surrounded by talented and radical young intellectuals who represented ideas, tendencies and aspirations that had been fermenting in the frustrated middle classes for a long time.

The elections of 1910 were a triumph for the new Liberal Party. Venizelos formed his first cabinet, which consisted almost entirely of new men. A period of intense reconstruction and radical reform thus began. The bourgeois intellectuals would attempt what they had been dreaming of for a long time: the construction of a modern democracy on the Western European model.

The prerequisite for the reform programme of the Liberals was a constitutional reform. The constitution of 1864 was fully revised, individual liberties guaranteed, and the foundations of a 'State of Law' were laid. However, though some of the formal prerogatives of the monarchy were curtailed, the real powers of the King remained ambiguous, a fact which was to have explosive consequences.

On this institutional framework, Venizelos launched an impressive legislative programme. Land reform was the most urgent and difficult problem. A constitutional amendment (1911) was promulgated authorizing expropriation with compensation – though not without bitter opposition from the still powerful landowner class. The medieval agrarian system of the Ionian islands was abolished (1912) and agricultural co-operatives were formed for the first time. Social legislation was equally radical. Low wages were exempted from confiscation in cases of debt (1909), the trade union federations of Athens and Piraeus were recognized (1910), Sunday was made a compulsory rest day (1910), a new and rapid procedure was introduced for the adjudication of disputes between workers and management (1912), joint unions between workers and employers were forbidden (1914), and the newly established unions of workers were permitted to negotiate and sign collective labour contracts. Finally a compulsory general labour insurance scheme was introduced in 1914.

The fiscal system was also reorganized on a more equitable basis. Progressive taxation of income was introduced in 1911 and death duties were reorganized and greatly increased in 1914. If, however, the legislative framework set up by Venizelos's government was unprecedented in scale and progressive in outlook, some of this legislation took many years to bear fruit. For example, bitter opposition from the landowners ran parallel to Venizelos's own hesitancy in the adjournment of effective land redistribution, a fact which, later on, contributed to the abandonment of Venizelos by large masses of peasants whose aspirations he had not lived up to. For the time being, however, the shortcomings of Venizelos's policy were not yet apparent. The new spirit he had managed to convey in all sectors of governmental activities had given the country a new self-confidence.

It should be stressed that the reinforcement of the country's military forces had also received the highest priority. Under British and French supervision, both the Army and Navy were fundamentally reorganized and strengthened. Thus, when the Balkan Wars of 1912–13 broke out, Greece, under Venizelos, found herself strong enough to cope with them. First in coalition with Serbia, Montenegro and Bulgaria against Turkey and subsequently with Serbia against Bulgaria, the Greek Army was victorious. Crown Prince Constantine led the Greek armies into Salonica, and after the treaty of Bucarest (1913), which put an end to the wars, Greece acquired Crete, Epirus, most of Macedonia (including Salonica) and the Aegean islands, except for Imbros and Tenedos, the two gates to the Hellespont straits.

But this triumphant hour of Hellenism was not to last long. Constantine, who ascended the throne after the murder of King George by a madman, soon quarreled with Venizelos, against whom he had borne a personal grudge since the First Balkan War. He quickly assembled around him the remnants of the old political world and, basing himself on the Army, in which he had been idolized since the victorious and flamboyant campaigns he had led, he indulged in a systematic sabotage of the Prime Minister's policies. From then onwards, there were two rival centres of political power.

When the First World War broke out in 1914, diplomatic considerations added to the undercurrents of strife that had been lurking between the two men. Constantine, who was married to the Kaiser's sister, was strongly pro-German. But he could not openly press towards entering the war on the central powers' side, as both Turkey and Bulgaria, the main enemies of Greece, were on the German side already. He therefore opted for neutrality, which brought him to an open clash with Venizelos, who had decided to enter the war on the side of the Allies. Believing in the final victory of the Western powers, particularly in British naval supremacy in the Mediterranean, and hoping for further Greek territorial gains, Venizelos insisted on clinging to the Greek–Serbian alliance of 1913 according to which Greece should assist Serbia if the latter were attacked by Bulgaria. A Bulgarian attack against Serbia being imminent, Venizelos was for full cooperation with Britain and France, who were offering an alliance. The King, however, was adamant against it. Venizelos therefore resigned, but won the subsequent general election (1915) and was returned to office. Five months later, however, he was once more obliged to resign by the King's blatant refusal to accept the government's policy. Secretly the King had already been in touch with the Kaiser, and had even let the Bulgarian ambassador know that his country had nothing to fear from Greece whatever happened. This flagrant misuse of the King's constitutional authority led to Serbia being overrun, while Venizelos could do nothing except denounce the King and his duplicity. By now Constantine was reigning practically as a dictator through a series of puppet governments, and fierce repression against the Venizelists set in. Venizelos consequently refused to take part in the forthcoming election (1916) and pursued an extra-parliamentary opposition.

In the meantime the military situation of the Allies had become precarious. The Allied troops that had landed in Salonica could do little without Greece's aid or at least support, and the failure of the Gallipoli expedition made the opening of a Balkan front all the more urgent. On the other hand Constantine was under continuous pressure by his wife and the Kaiser to enter the war on Germany's side, or at least to remain benevolently neutral. In spite of all the Allied threats and interventions, he surrendered the strategic fort of Rupel on the Greco–Bulgarian border to the Bulgarians. In September he even authorized the Bulgarians to enter the port of Kavalla on the Aegean, and ordered the Greek division garrisoned there to surrender.

This convinced the Allies that more dynamic measures would have to be taken. Venizelos, who had departed in rage to his native island, was encouraged to proclaim a revolution, and to establish a rival government in Salonica (October 1916). Immediately, additional Allied troops landed in Salonica in great numbers. Anglo–French troops also landed in Athens with Constantine's grudging consent but were obliged to depart when the royal troops put up an unexpected resistance. Consequently a blockade was imposed and Constantine was finally obliged to abdicate in favour of his second son, Alexander (June 1917), thus enabling Venizelos to return to Athens in triumph.

This defined Venizelos's relation to the Allies and especially to Britain. Throughout his political career Venizelos was to adhere faithfully to his firm principle in foreign policy: his belief that Greece's interests are permanently associated with Britain, whose advice he never ceased to follow. His subsequent attitude towards the monarchy was to a very great extent dictated by Britain, whose only objection towards monarchy in Greece was in the person of Constantine. And when in the mid-thirties violent unrest seized the Cypriots, who demanded union with Greece (Cyprus was promised to Greece during the first war as it was later to be promised by implication during the second), Venizelos, who had fought for many years for the union of Crete with Greece, flatly refused to sponsor the aspirations of the Cypriot people. But this is looking forward.

A year and a half later, the war ended. The Allied victory enabled Greece to fulfil all her territorial desires. By the Treaty of Sèvres (1920), Western and Eastern Thrace, and the islands of Imbros and Tenedos, went to Greece, who was also entrusted with the administration of Smyrna and a large chunk of its Anatolian hinterland. The triumph of Venizelos's policy was total. But the price Greece had to pay was incommensurably large. The feud that had begun as a personal dispute between Venizelos and Crown Prince Constantine back in 1912 had by now developed into a national 'schism' of extreme bitterness that was to dominate the social and political life of the country between the two wars.

Persecution and open terrorism of opponents in both camps resulted in an insurmountable gap. The question of the regime, that is monarchy versus republic, blurred all other issues and superseded the grave social problems which had originally been its cause.

Foreign-policy issues dominated the 1920 general election. The Royalists, with the slogan of 'small but honourable Greece', preached demobilization and peace, while the Liberals campaigned for the new 'Greater Greece' spanning two continents and five seas. Eight years of continuous mobilization and fighting had had their effect on the war-weary people. While retaining his strength among the liberal bourgeoisie and the working class of the larger towns, Venizelos suffered a heavy setback among the peasants and lost the election. The unfortunate accidental death of King Alexander, a few weeks before the election, added to the difficulties by posing the problem of the succession. The Royalists, who formed the new government, held a plebiscite which led to the return of King Constantine – to the discomfort of the Allied powers.

The government was faced at once with the problem of enforcing the Treaty of Sèvres, which had created 'Greater Greece' at the expense of Turkey. Especially delicate was the situation in the hinterland of Smyrna, where the Greek administration had to cope with a hostile Turkish majority. Under the spell of the image of 'Greater Greece', the Royalists reversed their own platform and continued Venizelos's dynamic foreign policy. But – openly distrusted by the Allies, whose interests had by now switched – they were left alone against the tide of the new Turkish nationalism that was irresistibly rising under Mustapha Kemal's inspired leadership. The morale and efficiency of the Army had been greatly reduced by the purges of most Venizelist elements, so the attempt to launch a general offensive against Kemal's stronghold in Ankara ended in disaster. In August 1922, the Greek Army was smashed and fled in disorder before the Turks, who pursued its remnants into the sea, slaughtered thousands of Greeks, and finally set fire to Smyrna in the midst of indescribable chaos. Hundreds of thousands of Greeks were forced to flee to the neighbouring islands or the Greek mainland. It was the end of 2,500 years of Greek supremacy on the Aegean coast of Asia Minor – and of the 'Great Idea'.

This disaster was to have profound and lasting effects on the nation's life. The immediate result was a revolution, staged by a number of Republican officers under Colonel Plastiras. The King had to abdicate once more – this time in favour of his son, George II – and to go into exile, where he died a few months later. The revolutionary government and the Venizelists, now back in favour, carried out a new purge against members of the Royalist clique, who were held responsible for the disaster. Six of the most prominent personalities, including ex-Premier Gounaris, were executed after a summary trial. The 'schism' between Venizelos and Royalists had been sanctioned with blood, thus feeding fanatical controversies for two more decades.

The Asia Minor disaster led to the treaty of Lausanne (1923), which was to draw the final frontier of Greece.[2] Greece lost Eastern Thrace, the islands of Imbros and Tenedos, and, of course, Smyrna and the Anatolian provinces. Most important however was the clause stipulating the obligatory exchange of populations between Turkey and Greece. Over a million and a half Greeks were to be transferred from Anatolia to Greece. The enthnologic and political map of the Near East would be greatly modified.

Ten years of war had resulted in the creation of a country

2. Apart from the addition of the Dodecanese, which was ceded to Greece by the Italians in 1947.

totally different from what it had been before. Greek territory doubled[3] and the population grew even more spectacularly.[4] The 1,500,000 refugees, whose social and economic integration was to constitute the greatest and most urgent problem of the country, changed the population structure completely. The urban population was greatly augmented, especially in the Athens district and the few large towns, where a numerous urban proletariat was created for the first time.[5] Hundreds of thousands of refugees formed belts of misery around the main cities, unemployed, moneyless and homeless, thus creating a permanent furnace of social and political turmoil. Another important result of the flood of refugees, and the obligatory population exchange, was the complete transformation of the ethnic composition of Macedonia. The departure of the Moslems, and the deliberate policy of the Liberal governments who installed Anatolian peasants in the abandoned plots, resulted in the total domination of the Greek element in an area where ethnological heterogeneity had given rise to repeated international imbroglios.[6]

Yet, despite all these changes, Greece remained a predominantly agrarian country. So land reform was still the most urgent socio-economic problem, and the arrival of the refugees merely accentuated it. In the newly acquired provinces of Macedonia and Thrace, as in Thessaly earlier, the Ottoman feudal system of big estates prevailed. Fear of social

3. Rising from 63,211 square kilometres in 1912 to 130,199 square kilometres in 1922.

4. Rising from 2,631,952 inhabitants in 1907, to 5,016,889 in 1920 and 6,204,674 in 1928 after the refugee influx had been completed.

5. Thus while in 1908 only 24 per cent of the population lived in towns of over 5,000 inhabitants, the percentage had risen to 27 per cent in 1920 and to 33 per cent by 1928. Greater Athens grew from 452,919 inhabitants in 1920 to 801,622 in 1928.

6. Whereas in 1912 the Greeks represented only 42.6 per cent of the Macedonian population as opposed to 39.4 per cent of the Moslems, 9.9 per cent of the Bulgarians and 8.1 per cent of miscellaneous groups (especially Jews), by 1926 the Greeks had reached 88.8 per cent, the Moslems had all left, and the Bulgarians and Jews had fallen to 5.1 per cent and 6.1 per cent respectively. In Macedonia the refugees represented 45 per cent and in Thrace 35 per cent of the total population.

revolution and mounting refugee pressure combined to hasten and reform. Venizelos in 1917, and the revolutionary government in 1923, decreed the expropriation of practically all large estates (public, private or Church-owned) and their distribution to landless peasants.[7] However, resistance by the landowners combined with the slowness and inefficiency of the overstaffed and bureaucratic civil service to delay the process of reform, which was completed only in 1937. Thus the whole inter-war period was marked by the peasants' endless struggles to overcome legal, administrative and economic obstacles. This partly explains the vehemence with which Greek peasants clung to their privately owned small plots, and their reluctance to consider other, more radical solutions of the land problem. The very low ratio of arable land to total area, and the consequent rural over-population,[8] led to the creation of extremely small plots, totally insufficient for adequate subsistence.[9] The widespread parcelling-out of these plots added to the economic plight of the peasants.[10] The surplus population had been relieved by mass emigration to the United States, but this was drastically restricted by the new US immigration law of 1922.[11] Thus, agrarian under-employment was intensified and contributed, by keeping the capital–labour ratio extremely low, to perpetuating the very low productivity of agriculture.

There was another reason for the lack of any significant capital investment in agriculture: there were no large agricultural units of production to introduce modern techniques. Although collective cooperatives were introduced and

7. Ultimately over 1,200,000 hectares, amounting to 38 per cent of the arable land of the country, were thus distributed.

8. It was estimated that 50 per cent of the rural population was 'surplus', i.e. more than needed in view of the prevailing type of production.

9. Thirty-six per cent of the agricultural units were smaller than 10 hectares, 36 per cent were of 10–30 hectares, 24 per cent of 30–100 hectares, and only 4 per cent over 100 hectares.

10. In 1929, each peasant owned an average of 5.6 pieces of land, sometimes at considerable distances from one another. It has been estimated that the peasant produced enough to feed between 1.5 and 2 persons.

11. The yearly average of Greek emigrants to the USA was 25,000 between 1901 and 1910, and 12,000 between 1920 and 1930.

encouraged, they did not manage to dominate the scene. Small and middle-sized units, cultivated by the owner and his family, remained the norm. This impeded the creation of a separate class of landless agricultural workers,[12] and contributed to a pronounced conservatism of the peasantry which was to prove of great political significance.

The organization of agricultural credit could have functioned as an important impetus for the modernization of Greek agriculture. The scarcity of peasant-owned capital being forbidding, it was only through the state that the Greek peasants could hope to acquire the funds to purchase fertilizers and mechanical instruments that would lead to an increase in productivity. State credit was also needed to free them from the usurers, who, if they could not deprive them of the land, which was proclaimed to be under certain conditions unalienable, effectually squeezed them to the bone. But the creation of the Agricultural Bank in 1929 proved insufficient to cope with the problem. Though a large number of peasants profited from loans,[13] the Bank's funds were inadequate and the amounts lent were therefore far too small to finance a new productive structure. Thus, many peasants became economically dependent on the state and were always demanding moratoria or postponements for the small sums which they owed and could not repay. Hence in turn a political dependence of peasants on local politicians developed. To the present day, the relationship between peasants and representatives of the government has had feudal–aristocratic undertones. The peasant could hope for nothing better than a small loan, the abrogation of an old debt, or a moderately good price for his product.

The urban scene had also changed drastically after the war. The long years of fighting, the influence of the Russian Revolution, and especially the tragic conditions of the urban refugees, led the working class to organize on a more radical basis.

12. In 1928 only 6 per cent of the agrarian population was landless and worked as labourers of unowned land.

13. In 1932 one-fourth of land cultivators had been given loans, averaging 3,368 drachmas.

The General Confederation of Trade Unions was created in November 1918,[14] and the Greek Socialist Party a week later. In 1922 it adhered to the Comintern, and two years later it became the Communist Party of Greece. The rapid rise of proletarian consciousness necessarily had political repercussions. It contributed to the gradual ossification of the Liberals, who feared a more radical critique of the foundations of society, even if this critique did not, for a long time, take alarming dimensions in terms of the actual political forces that stood behind it. For despite the miserable economic conditions, the Communists failed to acquire a significant following among the refugees, and remained a marginal political force throughout the inter-war period. This can only be partly explained by the Comintern directive urging the creation of a confederate Balkan state, in which Macedonia and Thrace would be detached from Greece and form separate states (1924).

The main reason for the restricted appeal of the Communists must rather be sought in the social background of the majority of the refugees. Indeed, the bulk of the urban Anatolian Greek population, which had been transformed into a *lumpenprolateriat* around Athens had previously constituted the solid middle classes of the main towns of Asia Minor and Bulgaria. Despite their destitute condition, most of them had never relinquished their bourgeois mentality. They were also ably manipulated by the Venizelist officials during the long years when they fruitlessly waited for reparations, housing and status. It was only later on, and to the extent that they were gradually integrated as industrial workers in Greek society and had consequently abandoned their dream of reconquering the status they had lost, that they started to act and function as a working class. During the inter-war years of political and social upheaval the very destitution, in the midst of which they had created their little world of non-integrated petitioners, served as a brake for the social movement which their own situation had helped to create.

14. Representing 214 unions with 60,000 members, out of a total of 336 unions with 100,000 members.

Finally, it should be kept in mind that the industrial workers as a whole were still a small minority of the total population. Industry was mainly organized on a small scale, most enterprises employing under five workers.[15] Family-type organization also impeded the development of strong social movements except in the few large enterprises and in the public services. Although industry developed rapidly up to the Second World War, heavy industry never took root. The working class continued throughout the period to be numerically weak, for the most part unorganized, and to a significant degree under the patronizing influence of the employers. Greece was still an agrarian and underdeveloped country.

15. In 1920 out of 2,213 industrial units, employing a total of 130,777 workers, 1,188 employed between 1 and 5 workers, 743 between 6 and 25 and only 282 over 25 workers. In 1928 only 33 per cent of the population were salary or wage earners of any kind. Sixty-one per cent worked on their own account and 6 per cent were employers. In the same year 68 per cent still worked in primary production, 15 per cent in industry of all kinds, mines and transport, and the remaining 17 per cent in trade, public services and services of all kinds. It is finally significant that notwithstanding the large and over-swollen civil service, only 5.5 employees, workers and wage earners correspond to 1 employer.

CHAPTER 3

The Failure of Democracy (1922–40)

THE military revolution of 1922 saved the country from the total chaos that had resulted from the Asia Minor *débâcle*. The radical officers who had assumed control managed to reorganize the Army and impose discipline within a very short period of time, thus discouraging the Turks from continuing an aggressive policy. The Treaty of Lausanne (1923), the negotiation of which was again carried out by Venizelos, consolidated the peace. But the intense political feud between Royalists and Venizelists was to take on disastrous dimensions. The anti-dynastic fervour of the revolutionary government, which had been only slightly moderated after the dethroning of Constantine, was intensified after an unsuccessful army putsch under General Metaxas, the only Royalist leader still free (October 1923). As a result of that putsch the question of monarchy or republic was open again. But the Venizelists themselves were by now splitting. In the absence of Venizelos, who (except for one brief period) did not return to active politics until 1928, the lack of any other undisputed leadership enabled the centrifugal forces which had been lurking to manifest themselves acutely. The Left, under Papanastassiou, who represented a continuation of the radical, mildly socialist, movement which had emerged during 1909, and was quickly swallowed by the Venizelist tide, sided with the vehemently anti-Royalist officers against the bulk of the Liberals, who were following Venizelos's instructions. He, again deferring to British wishes, was reluctant to contemplate any change of regime. This split had serious repercussions on the subsequent evolution of the Liberals. The Republicans did not win a majority in the elections of December 1923, which were won by the moderate Liberals after a Royalist abstention; but, two days after the election, an ultimatum of the Revolutionary Committee representing the army obliged King George to leave the country. A republic was proclaimed on 25 March 1924 and ratified by a subsequent plebiscite (13 April 1924). But the flagrant intervention of the Army on behalf of a political faction, particularly regarding an issue which could and should have been settled by popular vote, was to have lasting effects on political life. It inaugurated a series of Army interventions, putsches and pronunciamentos which deeply disrupted the new republic's frail foundations.

Between 1924 and 1928 there were ten Prime Ministers, three general elections, and eleven military *coups* or pronunciamentos. A military dictatorship was imposed and subsequently overthrown by another military *coup*. The President of the Republic was deposed once and resigned twice, only to revoke his resignation. The active presence of the Army on the political scene imposed an unwanted alliance on the left-wing Republicans, now the only politically articulate force for progress. Thus, with the compliance of virtually the entire political world, a kind of parallel power was created, courted and recognized by all parties and factions. Greek politicians of every shade – having repeatedly intrigued with the Army, used it, and formed alliances with it – accepted it as the supreme arbiter, whose 'will' was a fully recognized part of the system. The very forces that had fought for a republic, and had finally succeeded (if by dubious methods) in creating it, now contributed to maintaining a permanent putschist tradition in the armed forces.

The turmoil was self-perpetuating, since the Army was naturally purged after each successful or unsuccessful putsch. The hundreds of purged officers, who were a powerful pressure group, or rather many pressure groups, wanted to get their commissions restored and were a constant source of unrest. Throughout the inter-war period the Greek Army remained the object of interminable strife between the factions who fought for its control.

If this putschist element in the Army remained for a long time dominantly anti-Royalist, and as a rule Republican, its very presence and menace undermined the structures it aspired to establish. Although the Republican form of the regime was not openly challenged for many years, it never succeeded in penetrating popular imagination as a permanent state of affairs. Thus, Army intervention was accepted as an intrinsic characteristic of Greek political life, and when, later on, a right-wing Royalist dictatorship was imposed by General Metaxas, the majority of the middle classes reacted, at least in the beginning and before its openly fascist character had become manifest, with more lassitude than outrage.

Another effect of the Army's interventionist tendencies was the gradual conservatism which was to permeate the progressive forces that had abandoned the Liberals in 1922. The progressives' alliance with the ultra-Republican generals on the issue of the republic finally led them to political subjugation to a military faction, whose radicalism was centred on unconditional opposition to the monarchy. The establishment of the republic naturally deprived the officers of the single issue which united them. Their interventionist threats were consequently devoid of any specific ideological or political content, and very soon they split into numerous factions, some of which subsequently turned Royalist in the indescribable chaos which was to prevail until 1928, when Venizelos, driven by his own uncontrollable ambition and by his successors' inability to unite themselves around a substitute leader, returned to active politics. The radical Republicans who had separated from the Venizelists in order to pursue a more progressive policy thus found themselves entangled in an alliance which was not based on any ideological or programmatic substance. In order to extricate themselves they had to choose their ground. But instead of trying to ally themselves with the nascent socialist labour movement which, if still very small, was now growing rapidly, they chose to return to a series of unstable coalitions with the Liberals, who were enabled to impose their conservative policies.

Important constitutional issues which dominated the political world until the republican Constitution was promulgated in 1927 contributed to the continuation of the alliance of Papanostassiou's left-wing Republicans with the Liberals. But the former's definite break with the nascent worker organizations had detrimental effects in the long run. The recently formed Communist Party stepped in and assumed the practical leadership of the labour unions. But the gap between them and the other progressive political forces quickly became wider, as the Comintern's relentless attacks against all shades of bourgeois parties (including all agrarian movements) not only prevented effective coalitions of progressive forces, but also greatly facilitated the open persecution they were subjected to from the day they were founded.

The first historic chance for the creation of a strong social-democratic movement had thus been lost. The protests of Papanastassiou against the domestic policies of the Venizelists became more and more feeble. By the beginning of the thirties, the 'Democratic Union' as the left-wing Liberals were called, had been transformed into a faction of the Liberal Party, totally subjected to the latter, and incapable of presenting a plausible alternative to Venizelos. But the disappearance of the Left implied that the remaining political groups were more or less in agreement about fundamental social issues. The gradual disappearance of the landowner class and of their political counterparts virtually eliminated policy differences between the Liberals and the Populists (Conservatives), the latter representing the forces that had developed out of the old Royalist clique. However, the schism between Venizelists and Populists was still so deeply entrenched, both in popular opinion and in the political world, that the antagonism between these two main groups remained alive even though the social causes that had given rise to it had long since disappeared. Thus, with the political struggle detached from reality, the issues which were truly significant were plunged into silence. The relative weakness of the labour movement, and the lack of any organized opposition from the Left, completely blurred the real social issues.

The middle classes, whose ascendancy had given rise to the Liberal movement, were by now strongly entrenched in the social and political structure. Industrial activities were still marginal, and throughout the inter-war period Greek finance capital was very reluctant to assume the task of domestic industrialization. This phenomenon, which is undoubtedly related to the international recession, should also be seen in the light of the specific historical context within which Greek capitalism evolved. This is a function of the development of European colonial interests in the Near East. The total decay of the Ottoman Empire and the Egyptian Khedivate during the latter half of the nineteenth century enabled the Western powers to impose upon them a quasi-colonial status. It was the Greek merchants and bankers who were the major beneficiaries of this development, and between 1880 and 1910 colossal fortunes were made in the Mediterranean periphery. If the 1922 crisis eradicated the Greek element from Turkey and Bulgaria, their position remained unchallenged in Egypt and to a certain extent in Rumania, where the most influential Greek financiers continued to make their fortunes. Typically, many of the closest advisers of Venizelos in the economic and banking field belonged to this group. This undoubtedly helps to explain Venizelos's automatic obedience to British and French diplomatic interests. It also provides a deeper understanding of the reluctance of Greek capital to centre its interests upon domestic development. While the political foundations of the 'Great Idea' had been completely destroyed, the international context enabled the Greek bourgeoisie to continue thriving beyond Greek frontiers. Thus the peculiar evolution of the Greek ruling class allowed the revival of some of the ideological tenets which had been created during the nineteenth century. Not surprisingly, therefore, the main preoccupation of the bourgeois liberals was a monetary stabilization which would enable merchant capitalism to develop undisturbed. A natural consequence of this was that the ruling classes came to cooperate equally with both the Liberals and the Populists.

The refugee influx, however, created an enormous problem of employment and social integration. Even though it represented a bonus of skilled labour, industrialization did not advance significantly. The Liberals were concerned with preventing the refugee movement from joining hands with the militant labour movement. The Communist Party, for its part, was unable to utilize the despair of the refugee masses, since it insisted on a dogmatic proletarian line, which was hardly acceptable to the bulk of the refugees whose hopes were deliberately flattered by the Liberals.

Thus when Venizelos returned to politics in 1928, to preside for four and a half years over the longest and most stable government of the inter-war period, the internal structure of the republic was already frail. His immense prestige, especially among the refugees, brought about a regroupment of the Liberal and Republican forces, while the Populists had not yet been able to recover from the revolution of 1922 and the discredit they had suffered after the Asia Minor disaster. Yet, despite the lack of any serious opposition, Venizelos was confronted by difficulties which rapidly proved unsurmountable. The integration of the refugees was the dominant economic problem. The extremely low productivity of agriculture only became graver when 800,000 additional farmers were added to an already overcrowded countryside. Huge capital investment was needed in order to develop new arable land and to finance the new farming units. Although a considerable additional arable area was brought into cultivation, productivity rose very slowly. Problems of readjustment of the uprooted peasants, the extremely bad crops of the years 1929–31 and the rapid fall in international demand for luxury agricultural products, which constituted Greece's main exports, contributed to the intensification of the agricultural problems and to the growing trade deficit.[1]

Equally urgent was the problem of housing the numerous refugees in urban areas. The aid of international capital was

1. Thus between 1929 and 1934 the gross trade of Greece declined by 21.5 per cent in quantity and by 70.5 per cent in prices. By 1934 exports had fallen to 280 million francs representing less than half the value of imports. The Greek export gap, which was created by the sharp fall in demand for tobacco and currants in 1929–32, was subsequently covered in part by the deliberate policy of Germany, who managed to create a zone of virtual German monopoly in trade, a fact that was to have considerable political significance in 1938. Germany imported 43 per cent of Greek exports, almost tripling the share of German trade before the First World War.

consequently sought and Venizelos's prestige was instrumental in securing large foreign loans, despite the world crisis. This, however, in combination with the Hoover moratorium on war indemnities, which Greece was due to receive, weighed heavily on the foreign debt. By 1932 it amounted to 100 dollars per person (more than the *per capita* income), and its servicing required between 40 and 50 per cent of the national budget. The international crisis worsened the impasse, and partial national bankruptcy was proclaimed in 1932, a fact which strengthened the pressure of foreign creditors.

Under these conditions rapid industrialization proved impossible. The dependence of Greek industry on imported capital goods aggravated the unfavourable trade balance. Private Greek capital was mainly oriented towards light industry on a very small scale. The only ventures of any importance were undertaken by foreign, mainly British, firms.[2]

Venizelos's failure to implement structural changes in the Greek economy finally led to his downfall. By then the liberal bourgeoisie, who constituted his main support, had become prematurely ossified, both socially and politically, and finding itself on the defensive against the rising tide of working class pressure. Naturally, this disarray found its political counterpart in the lack of a decided and firmly oriented leadership. The failure of Venizelos and the crisis that followed only aggravated the confusion of the leading strata. Hence renewed Army interventions and prospective 'strong men' were not universally deplored, and parallel centres of decision in the Army and the political system were allowed to evolve almost independently of one another. The return of Venizelos in 1928 had only temporarily averted the political crisis. His downfall four years later precipitated it.

The inconclusive results of the 1932 elections, which brought the fall of the Liberal government, had another effect of key

2. This was only a prelude to what was to become one of the fundamental characteristics of the Greek economy after the Second World War. While enormous Greek-owned capital was profitably invested abroad, lack of capital in the country obliged (and still obliges) Greece to depend on foreign capital to fill the gap.

importance. For the first time the Communist votes exceeded 5 per cent, which, added to the 6 per cent of the newly formed Radical Agrarian Party, gave rise to considerable panic. During 1932 a large number of strikes[3] had been met by growing police violence, and the persecution of left-wing elements and labour leaders was intensified on the basis of a law of totalitarian inspiration 'For the Protection of the Social Regime', passed by Venizelos in 1929. Although the labour movement was still lacking in organization, unemployment (by 1934 there were 180,000 unemployed) had taken on alarming dimensions. The situation in the countryside was no better. The tobacco workers in Macedonia and the currant producers in the Peloponnese had been deeply affected by the international economic crisis which had curbed the demand for their products. Numerous agricultural demonstrations were violently dispersed and, until 1933, unrest among the peasants was continuous.

The shift towards the Populists that had taken place in the 1932 elections was a sign that the Liberal star was fading. Popular discontent and the fierce demagogic attacks of the Populists led to a temporary stalemate between the two main political groups. After many months of unstable coalitions, during which the in-fighting reached new heights, the Populists managed to form a government under Tsaldaris (1933), and the idea of restoring the monarchy was revived for the first time in many years. The worsening climate was marked by an attempt on the life of Venizelos and by government efforts to shield police officers who appeared to be implicated. A new paroxysm was set off by an unsuccessful Venizelist *coup* led by General Plastiras. A wave of purges against Venizelists in the Army and the civil service was inaugurated. Both major groups were contending for control of the Army, creating their own organizations within it and making no secret of their eventual intention to proclaim a dictatorship. The struggle was sharpened by growing international tension and the need to strengthen the Army. Hitherto, under the pressure

3. In 1932 there were 200 strikes involving 80,000 workers. Twelve thousand persons were arrested and 2,203 were sentenced to prison.

of Greek and British conservative circles, Venizelos had preached a policy of reconciliation; but now this was doomed. His personality and the symbolic connotations of his name defeated his intentions. The Populists, now in power, were steadily infiltrating and taking over the state machinery which had been in the hands of their opponents for twelve years. Having lost one election, the Liberals now realized that they were being ejected from the Establishment and began to fear their permanent exclusion.

The Venizelist answer came with the military *coup* of 1 March 1935. A part of the Army, still vehemently republican, proclaimed a revolution with Venizelos's blessing. Its suppression under the able direction of Kondylis, an ex-Venezelist General who had turned Royalist, marked the end of the Liberals' power. Over 1,000 officers were purged from the Army, some being executed. The civil service was thoroughly cleansed and Venizelos left the country, this time never to return.

The Populists were thus firmly entrenched. The Liberals' abstention in the next election (June 1935) merely intensified the terrorism practised against Venizelists, ex-Republicans and of course Communists.[4] The ultra-Royalists now had complete control of the armed forces. Feeling that the Populists were too moderate, they decided to act. The Royalist section of the Army, under General Papagos, supported Kondylis and – through a pronunciamento – brought about the return of King George II against the will of Tsaldaris, the Populist Prime Minister. A farce of a plebiscite was held, rigged to the extent that the votes recorded were much in excess of the registered number of voters. It was announced that 98 per cent of the electorate had opted for the monarchy. George promptly arrived on 25 November. The republic was no more.

The Liberals reacted mildly. Having lost control of the state apparatus, and subjected to continuous pressure by the British,

4. A sample from the anti-Venizelist press of the time is significant: 'Venizelos, son of the Devil, grandson of Beelzebub, great-grandson of Eosphorus, great-great-grandson of Satan. A well-known maniac injected with rage. He married a viper.'

Venizelos decided to support the King. In Venizelos's eyes, the King could serve as a symbol for the reconciliation of the two big political forces, a reconciliation which he had been urging in vain since the 1920s. Also, as titular head of the armed forces, the King could put a brake on the putschist tradition in an Army now totally controlled by the Royalists. In this new world, Venizelos hoped to emerge as the natural leader. The bulk of the Liberals followed their chief.[5] Only a fraction of the Venizelist forces, among whom were Papanastassiou and Papandreou, defied Venizelos's instructions. But neither they nor the Communists, who also reacted vigorously, had the strength or the following to influence the course of events.

The restoration of the monarchy paved the way to dictatorship. Contrary to Venizelos's hopes, the King did not act as a peacemaker between the rival forces. True, he immediately got rid of Prime Minister Kondylis (who had organized the rigged plebiscite), announced an amnesty and appointed a non-party government under Professor Demertzis. But he did not manage to free himself from the tutelage of the military clique which had put him on the throne. The ensuing general election (1935) was inconclusive. Neither party won an absolute majority, and the balance was held by fifteen Communist members. When a secret agreement between the Communists and the Liberal leader Sophoulis came to light, the Army – under Papagos – declared that it would not tolerate a government resting on Communist votes. Sophoulis gave in and supported another 'extra-parliamentary' government under Demertzis (March 1936). But the Vice-Premier and Minister of War was General Metaxas, leader of the unsuccessful coup of 1923, and well known ever since 1915 for his totalitarian

5. Significantly, no trouble arose in the Army. The purge had been complete and effective. From now on, except for a short period in the Second World War, the Army was to be ultra-Royalist to the core. The effects of the purge that followed the 1935 *coup* were permanent. A national Army had become a royal Army. The bulk of the officer corps, who in their own way had fought for years for the republic, were rendered impotent. But they had one more role to play in history: they made up almost the whole of the trained personnel in the resistance to German occupation in 1943–4.

ideas. On 13 April Demertzis suddenly died, and was promptly replaced by Metaxas. Almost the entire political world challenged the legitimacy of the King's choice, but in vain. Populist and Liberals began at long last to discuss forming a coalition, but took no immediate action. A strange coincidence transformed the political picture: Venizelos, Tsaldaris, Kondylis and the two ex-Presidents of the Republic, Koundouriotis and Zaimis, all died within a few months, leaving the arena open for all kinds of readjustments.

It has been suggested, but not yet proved by written evidence, that the King's choice of Metaxas was favoured by the British, obliged by the death of Venizelos to find a new strong man in Greece. Events were hastened by an internal crisis. In May 1936, a general strike in Salonica was suppressed with unprecedented brutality. Thirty workers were killed and over 300 wounded by Metaxas's police. A nation-wide general strike was therefore proclaimed for 5 August. Metaxas seized his chance: hundreds of labour leaders were arrested and deported. The Populists and Liberals made up their minds to react. On 22 July, they announced that they had agreed to form a coalition government and asked the King to dismiss Metaxas, who did not enjoy the confidence of Parliament. They would wait until October, however, for their new government to take office. But it was already too late. On 4 August, Metaxas proclaimed martial law and suspended the main provisions of the constitution. Monarchy had been transformed into Crown-sponsored dictatorship.

The hesitant and ambivalent policies of the Liberals during the Restoration crisis had sapped the potential for a vigorous resistance. Most Liberal leaders had repeatedly shown their implicit distrust of parliamentary government. Venizelos had asked for a non-party government; Papanastassiou had urged 'collective government', favouring a constitutional amendment to oblige the parties to coalesce and govern in co-operation; even Plastiras, the leader of the 1922 revolution, had often praised the powerful and vigorous Mussolini regime. As late as June 1936, Plastiras – who still enjoyed great prestige – considered a dictatorship by the present leader (Metaxas) to be the best solution. Venizelos's son Sophocles, a future Premier, even agreed to work with Metaxas in imposing totalitarianism 'for a limited period'.

So it is not surprising that neither Liberals nor Populists tried to rouse popular resistance to Metaxas. Protests were addressed to the King; all hopes of changing the situation were vested in his good intentions. The death of Papanastassiou in November 1936 deprived the Republicans of their last dynamic leader. It was only by the middle of 1937 that serious resistance was envisaged by a number of Republican politicians. By that time it was too late, since Metaxas had secured complete backing from the King and had established a fascist state structure which had seriously narrowed the margin of possible activities.

Thus the only organized force that tried to react to dictatorship was the Communist Party. But the systematic persecutions they had been subjected to since March had seriously affected their capabilities. Unsuccessful in bringing about a general uprising of the non-Communist democratic forces, and too weak to hope to overthrow the regime on their own, they were persecuted pitilessly by the growing secret police. According to an estimate of Metaxist propaganda, 50,000 'Communists' were eventually arrested and deported. Four and a half years of relentless persecution resulted in the Communists' underground organizations being virtually smashed. If a few small cells managed to survive, they were no threat to the dictatorship. It was only after the defeat and the German occupation had shattered the repressive mechanism of the dictatorship and had allowed the Communist leadership to emerge from prisons and concentration camps that an efficient organization was rapidly rebuilt. For the time being, what was left of them was obliged to remain hidden and ineffective. All forces that could potentially be effective had been neutralized. The 'Third Greek Civilization' was there to stay.

Metaxas's state was above all a police state. Though the dictator did not totally control the armed forces, who remained on the whole faithful to the King, he completely reorganized the police and security services on a fascist model.

He packed the civil service with his own people, imposed a rigid censorship on the press and plunged the country into an unprecedented obscurantism.[6] Concentration camps, torture, abolition of civil liberties, outlawing of labour unions, abolition of the agrarian federations and systematic persecution and imprisonment of dissidents effectively silenced all opposition.

The domestic policy of Metaxas was absolutely haphazard. His confused demagogy was based on a combination of moralistic, mildly socialist tenets with open totalitarian elements. In his *Plan for a Regime* he wrote:

> Two important matters:
>
> I. The form of society. A labour society. No Greek is allowed not to work. All non-workers who live out of their revenues shall be deprived of their political rights. They shall be, from the point of view of civil law, under tutelage. Labour can consist in spiritual work. But work it must be. Except for the unemployed, the old and the sick.
>
> II. Ownership. It shall be considered as a function within society.... Ownership and freedom of wealth exist, but they shall obligatorily be for the good of the collectivity. That means that the State can take wealth over when it is not administered for the good of the collectivity.

To this confused populism is added undiluted chauvinism. The youth organizations are told:

> What are the aims of this organization? King! King! Country! Religion! Family! Rebirth of Greece and the Fourth of August Regime! This latter point, the fourth of August regime, I underline, because it is the security, the vigilant safeguard of the others. When we did not have it, when we did not have the Fourth of August regime, you saw to what depths fell Monarchy, religion, country, family and all.

For all his demagogy, Metaxas could not solve the burning problems of the country. He seriously tried to promote the measures inaugurated by the Liberals for the improvement of both the workers and the peasants' conditions. But he sadly failed. Having suppressed all free expression of the trade-union movement, he raised minimum wages, enforced an

6. Huge book-burnings were organized and the works of Heine, Shaw, Freud, Zweig, France, Gorki, Dostoevski and Darwin were banned, among others. The Greek classical theatre was censored and Sophocles' *Antigone* was outlawed.

eight-hour working day, gave the workers a two-week annual vacation and took various other measures for the benefit of the working classes. But these measures were never implemented by the employers. The ban on strikes made all actual protest ineffective; and the growing dependence of the regime on industrial capital struck from Metaxas's hands the weapons which he had probably intended, originally at least, to use.

Employers, in fact, did well out of Metaxas. Though the built-in structural defects of Greek industry were intensified, private profit soared. The increase in wages was counterbalanced by the fall in the value of the currency, while taxation was reorganized to favour the richer classes. Indirect taxation made up 79 per cent of state revenue, and direct taxation was often not paid because of the corruption of the many-headed administration. It has been estimated that annual profits during this period reached a record 25 per cent return on capital. (Linardates, *I Tetarti Augousto,* p. 128).

The policies of the dictatorship did not earn the regime significant popular support. The urban workers, the middle classes and the peasants, whom Metaxas had hoped to win over by demagogy, were gradually driven into open antipathy to the regime. The inequality of income distribution was by now unbearable.[7] The hopes of a development that might modify the intolerable conditions of the lower classes had been completely dissipated and by 1940 it was only big capital, domestic and foreign, that supported the dictatorship.

A fascist ideology, corresponding to the nationalistic chauvinism of the petty bourgeoisie to which Metaxas himself be-

7. According to Professor Evelpides, income distribution in 1938 was as follows (113 drachmas = 1 US dollar):

Income in drachmas	*Number of families*
under 20,000	630,208
20,000 – 40,000	632,768
40,000 – 80,000	271,404
80,000 – 140,000	66,897
140,000 – 280,000	31,173
280,000 – 500,000	6,048
500,000 – 1,000,000	2,602
over 1,000,000	900

longed, was rapidly imposed as the official doctrine. The *Führerprinzip* of the infallible leader was proclaimed by Metaxas's propaganda. But the leader was a man who in twenty years of active political life had never succeeded in capturing the public imagination and remained the head of an insignificant parliamentary faction. The classic arsenal of totalitarian governments laws was made use of. A huge propaganda apparatus, youth organizations, radio, manipulated press and impressive public festivities sang the virtues of the 'Third Greek Civilization' and its leader. The centralized state and para-military organizations that were thus formed created the basis for the strong ultra-right movements that would play an important role later on.

Metaxas himself gives the best account of the regime:

> Since August 4th Greece has become an anti-communist anti-parliamentary, totalitarian State. Its agrarian and labour foundations make it anti-plutocratic. Thus, if Hitler and Mussolini were really fighting for the ideology they preach, *they should be supporting Greece with all their forces*. They should even acquiesce if immediate interests or geographical necessities had brought Greece nearer to England. However, on the contrary, Greece has remained distant from England. Except for the indispensable and necessary friendly relations, Greece has promised or given no help to England.

This speech, delivered on the eve of Germany's attack on Greece, illustrates the deep ideological affinity of Metaxas to fascism and Nazi Germany. But the pressure of King George and, above all, the economic dependence of Greece on Britain had made an open alignment of Greece with the Axis impossible, and Metaxas was obliged to give in completely to British demands. He agreed to an increase in the interest payments to British creditors (after personal intervention by the King) and offered unprecedented advantages to British firms operating in Greece. In his own words:

> I think the difficulties encountered by British firms in Greece (which they are complaining about) are really imaginary. One can really state that *the only favoured firms in Greece are the British ones*.... The British in Greece have a special kind of feeling, which they do not have when they discuss in Turkey or Yugoslavia and thus, their affairs in those

countries are often solved *according to the interests of the countries and not according to the interests of the British entrepreneurs.*

If, however, British capital had achieved considerable advantages in Greece, Germany remained the most important customer for the main Greek exports. The prices offered by England were extremely low compared to those paid by the Germans, who were fighting for the political control of the Balkans. A large loan was offered on moderate terms and Goebbels, Schacht and von Schirach visited Greece and were given fabulous receptions. This double economic dependence in an international context that was rapidly approaching crisis created great tensions within the regime. Thus, when the Second World War broke out, Metaxas attempted to follow a policy of neutrality. But the regime's internal contradictions between pro-Germans and pro-British had been resolved in Britain's favour. The King still controlled the Army and thus decided foreign policy. On the eve of the war, the Army headquarters were purged of some elements whose allegiance to the British cause was doubtful and General Papagos, who enjoyed the full confidence of the King and the British, remained Chief of Staff.

The growing Italian menace, as well as the fact that Hitler was demanding the abdication of King George, hastened a decision. Metaxas had no other choice but to opt for the British. An agreement was accordingly signed between the Greek and British staffs in view of an eventual Axis attack. Fascist Greece had been driven by necessity to the side of the democracies.

CHAPTER 4

Resistance (1940–44)

THE occupation of Albania by Mussolini (April 1939) extended the European crisis to the Balkans. Greece could scarcely hope to escape the general conflict that was obviously approaching. Relations with Turkey had been stabilized by the Treaty of Montreux (1936), but the hostility of both Italians and Bulgarians on the northern frontiers presented a growing threat. Metaxas had already strengthened the armed forces as much as possible, while also exercising maximum prudence to avoid being drawn into war. He even went to the limits of appeasement and refrained from accusing Italy when a Greek cruiser was torpedoed by an Italian submarine in the harbour of Tinos on 15 August 1940. But it was all in vain. On 28 October Mussolini issued an ultimatum and, without waiting for its rejection by Metaxas, ordered his troops to cross the Albanian border. Greece was in the Second World War.

Against all odds, the keenness of the Army and unanimous popular support enabled Greece to win the first victory chalked up against the Axis. Not only was the Italian offensive successfully held, but a series of energetic counter-attacks forced the Italian Army to retreat. By the end of the year, the front had been pushed back sixty kilometres into Albanian territory; sixteen Greek divisions had immobilized twenty-seven Italian, despite the crushing supremacy of the latter in equipment, artillery and aircraft.

The Greek Army's heroism and tenacity was, however, insufficient to resist a second attack by Germany. After the collapse of Yugoslavia, on 6 April 1941, the Germans, aided by their Bulgarian allies, launched a major attack across the Bulgarian border. The Greek Army, aided by a handful of British and New Zealand troops, could not possibly resist the Wehrmacht tide for long. The Germans were already beginning to break through when General Tsolacoglou, a future Quisling

Prime Minister, capitulated on 23 April.[1] King and government left the country and on 27 April the Wehrmacht entered Athens. Metaxas had been spared the end. He had died a few weeks before the German attack, having for the first time achieved a certain popularity with the aura of the Albanian victory. Except for Crete, the country was under Axis power. The dictatorship had been replaced by an incomparably more ignominious foreign occupation.

With the fall of Crete (May 1941) the whole of Greek territory came under Axis occupation. The Ionian islands were officially annexed by Italy, Eastern Macedonia and Thrace by Bulgaria, while the rest of the country was divided into German, Italian and Bulgarian occupation zones.

The situation in both annexed and occupied regions very soon grew disastrous. The functioning of the Greek economy was of no concern to the occupying powers. As there were no important factories to contribute to their war effort, the collapse of the country's economic life left them indifferent. Greece was forced to pay colossal sums for 'occupation expenses'. Besides, all the country's resources were taken over by the occupiers, who introduced special occupation banknotes, issued freely and without limits by all military units 'according to their needs'. This led to the immediate explosion of the monetary system. International trade was completely halted,[2] which was bound to lead to tragic consequences for a

1. Although all the circumstances of the collapse of the Greek front before the German attacks are still not clear, the defeatist tendencies in the administration and the pro-German feelings of a large number of officials and generals had been notorious. It was the Commander of the Northern Army, General Tsolacoglou, who formed the first Quisling government; the director of the Athens police had autographed pictures of Hitler and Goebbels hung next to Metaxas's and the King's. And the Defence Minister, Papadimas, had given Easter leave to the men holding the Centre front, where German pressure had been mostly felt (Stavrianos, *American Dilemma and Opportunity*, p. 57). It seems that the suicide of Premier Korizis, who had succeeded Metaxas, was closely related to his incapacity to control the state apparatus in an attempt to oppose the Germans by force.

2. Imports in 1941 were 6 per cent of the 1939 figure, 7 per cent in 1942, and 12 per cent in 1943. Exports in these years stood at 8 per cent, 6 per cent, and 3 per cent.

nation that was a heavy importer of foodstuffs. Naturally, goods vanished within a few weeks and the black market thrived. Very soon, the urban population was confronted with a food shortage. By the end of the year, it became famine. During the tragic winter of 1941–2, almost 300,000 people died. Probably more than defeat and foreign occupation, the horror of hunger – combined with the atrocities committed by the occupation forces – cemented the will of the Greek people. Their ultimate expendability led them to struggle, not to passivity. If they were to survive they had to resist. The question mark was against organization and leadership.

The Greek government-in-exile was completely cut off from the country. The lack of all communication led by degrees to the existence of two Greeces, completely different in aspirations, aims and structure. From 1941 to 1944 the ministers of King George II, occasionally reinforced by new political personalities who escaped from the homeland, lived and functioned within their own small world, which was more a continuity symbol they wanted to cling to than anything else. Even the Greek armed forces in the Middle East served under Allied HQ. The government's authority was thus purely nominal and its prestige at home was very low (mainly because of the role played by King George during the Metaxas dictatorship), even though it was gradually purged of its ex-fascist members. The weak politicians of whom it was made up, remnants of the pre-Metaxas political world, evoked nothing but indifference if not open mistrust.

New centres of power, new leaders, new mass movements and political aspirations were needed in the struggle that was about to begin, and the exiled government was incapable of providing them. The Greece of 1940, in terms of which they thought and acted, was nearer to that of 1920 than to that of 1942. Moreover, most of the old politicians – who had not been in the limelight since 1936 – were too hesitant or too cowardly to take the initiative in a clandestine reorganization of the national forces. Under the circumstances, it is only natural that the Communist Party should step in and fill the political gap. Most of the party 'cadres' had managed to escape prison upon the collapse of the Metaxist state, and their spirit of resistance and sacrifice matched the pugnacious mood generated in the Greek people by the German invasion. Their organizational experience in clandestine work and their simple attitude towards the ordinary people whom they addressed in their own language were great assets in the struggle that was about to begin, when the first nuclei of resistance were formed by the Communists. Tito's partisans had already started active resistance since July 1941, and news spreads fast in the Balkans.

Thus, as early as the beginning of 1942, resistance was beginning to take massive form. Of all the occupied countries of Europe, only in Greece and Yugoslavia did the resistance movement have the character of a universal popular outburst which would in due course result in a direct confrontation of military forces with the enemy. The high and virtually inaccessible mountain ranges in Greece enabled the guerrillas to operate from secure bases.

The first resistance organization had been founded as early as 28 September 1941, when the Communist Party (KKE) in collaboration with various smaller parties created the National Liberation Front (EAM), under whose political authority the creation of a People's Army of Liberation (ELAS) was envisaged. The aims of EAM as expressed in its foundation statute[3] were to resist the occupation and to see to it that a new democratic regime should be established in Greece after the end of the war. In both these aims, EAM found itself in full accord with the overwhelming majority of the people. If the Communists who were the leading political

3. I. The liberation of our country from foreign occupation and the achievement of national independence.

II. The formation of a provisional government by EAM after the expulsion of the foreign invaders. This government's sole purpose shall be the holding of general elections under the system of proportional representation for the election of a Constituent Assembly.

III. In order to ensure that the people shall be in a position to decide effectively on the regime they desire, unhindered by any reactionary attempt to impose a solution contrary to the people's will, EAM and all organizations affiliated to it will crush any such attempt by all available means.

force of EAM had other long-term objectives, the introduction of socialism was never envisaged as an immediate aim. Throughout the occupation, and even in the midst of the bitter civil wars that were to take place, EAM never departed from the official line stated in its founding document. In the policy stated there, no basic difference existed between the aims of EAM and those of most of the other organizations that were gradually being formed. Both the National Republican Greek League (EDES) and the national and Social Liberation Movement (EKKA), the most important of these, were formed by officers of the Greek Army known for their Republican and anti-Royalist sentiments. But none of these organizations managed to establish itself on a broad national basis or to penetrate the popular imagination to a significant degree. Both the EDES stronghold in Epirus and the EKKA-controlled regions around Mount Parnassus were simply operational bases. But in most of the countryside EAM reigned almost unchallenged. A Free State was formed in the mountains with full cooperation from the peasants, whose traditional indifference was gradually transformed into whole-hearted participation in the common struggle. Modern and efficient institutions were set up in regions where, until a few months before, the economy had worked on a virtually self-contained basis and where the social structure was still to a large extent patriarchal and archaic. In the words of C. M. Woodhouse, a British agent parachuted into Greece with the main object of breaking EAM politically:

Having acquired control of almost the whole country, except the principal communications used by the Germans, they had given it things that it had never known before. Communications in the mountains, by wireless courier and telephone, have never been so good before or since; even motor roads were mended and used by EAM–ELAS... The benefits of civilization and culture trickled into the mountains for the first time. Schools, local government, law courts and public utilities, which the war had ended, worked again. Theatres, factories, parliamentary assemblies, began for the first time. Communal life was organized in place of the traditional individualism of the Greek peasant. His child was dragooned into the EPON (youth body), his nest-egg levied into EA (relief work), his caique commandeered to equip ELAN

(EAM's naval army). Followed at a distance by the minor organizations, the EAM/ELAS set the base in the creation of something that the governments of Greece had neglected: an organized State in the Greek mountains. (*The Apple of Discord*, pp. 146–7).

But not only did services function more efficiently. The Greek peasantry awoke to a new political consciousness through the creation of democratic state structures, which gave the people, for the first time in history, some power to decide their own destinies. The 'Code for Self-Government and Popular Justice', published by ELAS in December 1943, was the first attempt to implant truly democratic principles in the Greek countryside. The structure of power and representation was directed upwards, and freely elected members constituted the administrative bodies on the municipal, country and regional levels. Justice was administered by elected judges and new penal and civil codes were issued in accordance with the long traditions of Greek mountain people.

Yet, despite the socialist inspiration of EAM, the reforms outlined above were radical only in so far as they aimed at giving the peasants a place in society. Notably, there were no provisions either to facilitate or to preclude any kind of land redistribution – still less collectivization. The land reform put in hand by the Liberal governments of the twenties and thirties had been completed under Metaxas, and the petty private ownership prevailing in the Greek countryside was a conquest dear to the bulk of the peasantry. Because the percentage of landless agricultural workers was small, the creation of a separate peasant-proletarian class had been impeded; and the shortcomings of the small and scattered agrarian units had not yet been seen as insurmountable. The 'Code for Self-Government' states: 'In no case can the courts order a land expropriation. They can, however, order the temporary installation of poor or landless peasants of the district, after fixing an equitable rent for the owner' (Article 65).

This was the nearest EAM got to socialist legislation. But if this reluctance of the Communists to proclaim a more radical programme can be explained by the specific conditions prevailing among the peasantry, it also explains the relative ease with which the unchallenged supremacy of EAM was shattered when, after liberation, the political battle took the form of open class struggle. The ideological penetration of the Communists during the occupation had been effected through the liberal-patriotic platform of the EAM coalition. The Communists had imposed their leadership, but not their ideology.

Whether or not these 'resistance' institutions could have functioned under normal conditions, there is no doubt that the archaic sub-cultures still prevailing in large parts of the country came into contact, for the first time, with a democracy that meant more than a vote in general elections. Yet this encounter was too brief, and too impregnated with the special and external phenomenon of national resistance, to leave permanent traces in the peasant outlook. After the defeat and destruction that befell the left-wing forces, the peasants returned for two more decades to their pre-war passivity.

Meanwhile, the resistance grew steadily in scope and intensity. Except for the towns and the main communication artery from Athens to Salonica, the whole country was controlled by the partisans by 1943. Nine enemy divisions were pinned down on garrison duty and were continually harried by the Greeks, who – by almost daily raids, sabotage, and later by regular battles – made the Balkan route for supplying the Afrika Korps with ammunition and material almost unusable. The most eloquent report comes from the Germans themselves:

Political situation in Greece, July 1943

Ninety per cent of the Greeks today are unanimously hostile to the Axis powers and are ready for open revolt. The EAM with its combat organizations is the main bearer of the entire resistance movement against the Axis powers. The greater part of the bands is subordinated to it. It is in a leading position politically speaking, and because it is very active and enjoys a coordinated leadership, it represents the greatest danger to the occupying forces. (quoted by N. Svoronos, *Histoire de la Grèce moderne*, p. 116).

Very soon, however, the first signs of strife between the Greek resistance movements became manifest. It is both impossible to ascertain and also, perhaps, irrelevant, whether it was the Communits or the non-Communists that were the cause. They both had good reasons to fear one another. The non-Communist organizations were obviously ill at ease with the fact that the Communist-inspired EAM had achieved undoubted political supremacy. Their chances of stopping the regime from slipping to the left after the war would be seriously curtailed if they did not succeed in establishing a military force equal or superior to ELAS. Thus, while they were originally democratically minded, their ill-disguised antagonism towards EAM gradually sent them into the arms of the British, and made them play the game of the King. On the other hand the EAM leadership was also increasingly hostile towards the other organizations, who challenged its power. A hostility that was in the beginning based on the mutual desire of each organization to strengthen itself on its own did eventually acquire specific ideological undertones. Thus, if EAM's attitude was until the end of 1942 one of extreme reserve, it developed into undisguised hostility as a result of the role of the British agents who were parachuted into Greece as liaison between the guerrilla forces and military headquarters in the Middle East. After an initial phase, during which the British had assisted all resistance organizations with weapons, supplies and money on a more or less equitable basis, they tried to strengthen the non-Communist organizations by every means, meanwhile preaching the paramount importance of unity and collaboration.

British policy should be seen in the light of the way in which the political problem of Greece was being treated. The King was still regarded as the only legal representative of the Greek people, although the regime remained for a long time an official continuation of the Metaxas dictatorship. On the death of the dictator, the King had unequivocally declared that 'all fields of activity, political and military ... as well as the organization of national youth, shall continue in the same spirit as before' (*New York Times*, 30 January 1941). And it was not until February 1942, almost a year after the country had been overrun, that George, obviously under strong pressure from the British, announced the official termination of the dictatorship.

Despite his dubious prestige and popularity, the King was the strongest British card in the political struggle that would inevitably followed the end of the war. Naturally, therefore, he was encouraged and pressed to broaden his representative capacity, while at the same time he refused to make any commitment that might in the future endanger his status. Naturally too in these circumstances, intolerable tension developed between EAM on the one hand and EDES and EKKA on the other. By 1943 the situation was explosive. Bitter battles were fought; and, notwithstanding the strong British pressure, each armistice was followed by new grievances and armed conflicts. The organizations accused each other of collaboration with the Germans. Although it appears to be untrue that any of the main organizations openly collaborated with the occupation forces – for, on all sides, the resistance was constantly growing both in dimension and in activity – it does seem to be true that Zervas, the leader of EDES, came into contact with the Quisling government behind the backs of his comrades in arms with a view to setting up a Greek collaborationist force, which would serve under the Germans against EAM. In the middle of 1943 Zervas, who had sworn allegiance to the King and was frankly playing the British game, was increasingly conscious of the implications of ELAS military supremacy. The creation of a well-armed group of collaborators called 'Security Battalions' suited both his own and the British purpose well. One more organized army group which would eventually fight EAM and secure, at least temporarily, the capital from an immediate takeover by the Communists could finally tip the balance. For meanwhile in Teheran Churchill had given up his plan for large-scale military intervention in the Balkans.

The British position was very delicate indeed. On the one hand they did not intend to let go their hold of Greece at any cost. The Empire was still alive, and Greece was an extremely important key to British predominance in the Eastern Mediterranean. On the other hand the war was still at a critical point and the strategic impact of the resistance in the Balkans was of fundamental importance. A direct clash with EAM was therefore out of the question until the end of the war. But the departure of the Germans would leave the ELAS in complete control of the country, including Athens. By 1944 ELAS had reached a force of 50,000 armed men stationed in the Athens–Piraeus region, while EAM membership was anything between 500,000 and 2,000,000 (out of a population of 7,000,000). Regardless of whether the Communists had in mind to attempt a take-over, the British would find themselves extremely weak. But, even after the war, military intervention without a pretext was (until the end of 1943 at least) not certain to be acceptable to Stalin. As Churchill's plan of large-scale military attack through the Balkans was finally turned down by both Roosevelt and Stalin, there seemed no other way for the British to avoid an undue increase of Communist influence in Greece than by creating a strong anti-Communist Greek military force that would see to it, if need be, that the Communist army was kept under control, or at least that a good pretext was given to the British for direct intervention.

Churchill is very explicit on the matter in his memoirs. On 29 September 1943 he writes:

> ... Should the Germans evacuate Greece we must certainly be able to send 5,000 British troops with armoured cars and Bren gun carriers into Athens .... The Greek troops in Egypt would accompany them .... Their duty would be to give support at the centre to the restored *lawful Greek Government. The Greeks would not know how many were coming behind them.* (Churchill, *The Second World War*, paperback edn, vol. 10, p. 188; italics supplied).

The contradiction between military and political considerations is manifest in the policy pursued. For a long time Middle East headquarters pursued different policies from those of the Foreign Office. It was only after the middle of 1943, when Churchill assumed personal supervision of the Greek problem, that the political considerations were placed above the short-term military objectives. Thus not only was the aid to the Greek left-wing guerrillas completely stopped; Churchill also backed the King in flatly refusing the demand of *all* the resistance organizations and of the exiled Greek government that he should not return to Greece before a plebiscite. This adamant restatement of the King's authority was complemented by the reinforcing of all military information that would eventually be used against EAM.

The British had thus to secure the allegiance of the two Greek brigades in the Middle East, where feelings between both officers and soldiers were mixed. This was far from easy: on the one hand there was a number of openly Royalist officers of fascist inclinations, distrusted because of their connexion with the Metaxas regime. They could obviously be trusted to play the monarchy's game but their influence was small. On the other hand, a significant number of officers and soldiers were openly sympathetic with EAM. They would have to be purged. But the majority of the Army were Republicans, distrusting both the Royalists and the Communists. Their attitude was mainly oriented towards maintaining discipline in the Army and refusing to accept any purge from the right or the left. This latter group was the strongest and their firm stand during the turbulent summer months of 1943, when a series of minor *coups* exploded from both the Royalist and the Communist sides, avoided a crisis. For the time being it was stalemate. But EAM still had a strong hold within the army, so that the army could not be counted upon in a crisis to comply with British orders.

Simultaneously, the strengthening of the non-Communist guerrillas on the mainland was pursued. But if the situation of these was problematic at the beginning of the occupation, by 1944 it had become extremely precarious. Although the British kept supplies pouring into them, the strategic advantage of ELAS remained overwhelming. And when, in September 1943, the Italians capitulated and surrendered to ELAS their weapons and supplies, the logistic supremacy of EDES and EKKA, which had been their only advantage, vanished into thin air.

The power of the Communists was indeed felt very quickly.

After a long series of bitter battles, EKKA was completely eliminated and its leader Psarros was murdered (April 1944).[4]

A large-scale military manoeuvre was simultaneously organized by ELAS against EDES. It was most probable that EDES would have followed EKKA's fate, but for the intervention of the Germans, who launched a massive attack against the ELAS, thus obliging them to retreat to the mountains. But if EDES was not eliminated it hardly counted any more as a countervailing fighting force, restricted as it was to a small area in Epirus.

British policy did not limit itself into the strengthening of the right-wing military forces. With considerable forethought, it was not the Royalist but the Republican and Liberal elements of the old political world that were encouraged and used. The main political forces with which the British were working in Athens, as well as the governments they finally installed in the Middle East, were not Royalist but Republican. The issue of the monarchy was ably played against these forces and the King was first unofficially pushed to assume an adamant position and then later unofficially pressed to give in to the Republican political forces that constituted the Greek government-in-exile. While, however, the Republicans were consciously or unconsciously playing the British game by focusing their attention on the royal issue which they finally were allowed to 'win' (as the King was obliged to give

4. Psarros's murder, which was to have great repercussions in the political *pourparlers* later on, still remains obscure. It seems sure that the orders did not come from the ELAS General HQ, and the murder was committed by men under the command of Aris Velouchiotis, one of the most redoubtable Communist guerrilla leaders who openly disagreed with the conciliatory line of the party and preached an immediate and violent take-over, to the exclusion of any negotiation with the government-in-exile, and the British. His strategy, which was nearer to Tito's conceptions, was never accepted by the Communist leadership. But as his following was great and his military prestige enormous, his uncompromising position greatly contributed to the vacillations of Communist policy, which could not afford to openly disown him. Psarros's murder should therefore be seen as one out of a series of fateful incidents through which the factions in the Communist leadership were creating *faits accomplis* in an attempt to impose their own policy on EAM/ELAS.

in and agree not to return before a plebiscite), the Greek Army was never put under 'governmental' control and remained under British authority. Finally it was purged not only of its Communist but of its Republican elements. But the Greek government was carefully kept predominantly anti-Royalist up to 1946.

By the beginning of 1944 it was obvious that the war was approaching its end. The situation in Greece looked ominous for British interests. For all her efforts, Britain had not achieved her main aim: the popular forces virtually occupied the whole country and there was no other Greek force that could possibly face them. The intensification of atrocities by the Germans, who in the last year of the occupation burned hundreds of villages and executed 70,000 people, had not broken the morale of the population. Victory, liberation and a new democratic Greece were near. The preponderance of ELAS was such that no civil war was feared. Even at that stage, it must be stressed, EAM still clung to its statutory aims: free elections and democracy. The bid for power seemed destined to take legal political forms. And truly political it was to be – at least in the beginning. Britain was about to score her last great political triumph, in the grand tradition of her invincible diplomacy. The uneducated, unsubtle leaders of EAM were no match for her.

CHAPTER 5

Liberation (March–December 1944)

ON 10 March 1944, the Political Committee of National Liberation (PEEA) was created by EAM in order to organize and direct the national struggle for liberation, to administer the regions already liberated and to ensure the people's sovereignty over the whole country. The PEEA included a considerable number of non-Communists and was presided over by Professor Svolos, the foremost Greek authority on constitutional law. It is significant that PEEA insisted, from the first day, on the democratic character of its structure and, before assuming its governmental functions, it went so far as to organize free elections by secret ballot throughout the country, held on 9 April 1944. The elected representatives constituted themselves into a national assembly which met in the village of Korischades in central Greece. Under the name of 'National Council' the assembly endorsed the authority of the PEEA and the latter became a representative government of Greece, working on Greek soil and backed by over a million votes. This was, in the words of Churchill, 'a direct challenge to the future authority of the Tsouderos government-in-exile. *An alternative communist-controlled Administration was thus formed as a rallying-point of all Greeks*' (italics supplied).

The effect of the creation of PEEA was indeed enormous. Following the example of Tito, the Greek resistance had manifested its intention of functioning as an organized political force in the shaping of post-war Greece. Even if the creation of a Communist state was not envisaged, it is clear that the return of the King without a previous plebiscite and the assuming of power by the puppet government-in-exile would not be tolerated. The balance of power was such that the authority of PEEA could not be challenged. Apart from the undoubted supremacy of ELAS on the mainland, the Greek brigades in Egypt were still very divided in their sympathies: 'They are very liable to be contaminated by revolutionary and Communist elements there. Satan finds some mischief still for idle hands to do' (Churchill, vol. 10, p. 192, 5 April 1944).

But the object of PEEA, as seen by its authors, unlike the object of the equivalent body that Tito set up in the Yugoslav mountains, was not to constitute a central governmental authority controlled by EAM to the exclusion of all other political forces. Not only was the ultimate fate of the monarchy left open; the authority of the government-in-exile was only challenged inasmuch as the latter was not fully representative of the Greek people, since it did not include members of the resistance organizations.

PEEA never went further than demanding the establishment of a national coalition government, in which their own representatives would be included, without however claiming the post of Prime Minister. This conciliatory attitude left room for considerable manoeuvring by the British. The removal of the issue to the level of a political argument on the composition of the future government gradually led to a change in the balance of power.

The same attitude had its military counterpart in the structure of ELAS. Unlike Tito's partisans, who were organized in the mountains on the massive basis of a popular army which was to constitute the main agent of the political struggle to come, the organized ELAS army was not the only preoccupation of EAM. The majority of EAM members were to remain in the towns acting as saboteurs and communication agents. These were the 'ELAS reserves', significantly more numerous than the popular army itself. The role of the reserves was to be mainly political in the narrow sense, in the future. The consequences of this strategy were twofold. First, the effective military strength of the ELAS troops was significantly weakened; this allowed the existence of other armed troops to contest their monopoly of power until the end of the occupation, and seriously impaired their bargaining power against the British. Second, it made the Communists more vulnerable within the towns themselves, because of their exposure to Germans and collaborationists and later to Royalists. The naturally more diversified town population was less prone to follow Communist leadership without question. Therefore, the broad coalition that constituted EAM had to be maintained. This explains the vacillating and contradictory strategy of the Communist leadership that was to lead to their defeat. True, the middle class had to a certain extent ceased to function as an autonomous interest group because of the economic collapse of the country, and had therefore on the whole accepted EAM leadership. Nevertheless, because the main EAM effort had been directed to a loosely organized city network, the social and economic patterns that had prevailed before the war were not shattered in the towns but had only temporarily ceased to function. Thus the liberation and the prospect of a rapid normalization of economic life contributed to the re-emergence of class differences that had been submerged during the war.

The first crucial turning point came as a result of PEEA's telegram to the Greek Premier Tsouderos, on 10 March 1944. After announcing its creation, PEEA stated that

> [our] main preoccupation is the creation of a government of national unity ... we are addressing ourselves to your Excellency, certain that you will comprehend the national necessities and that you will decisively contribute to the formation of a government of general national unity.

The impact of this demand on the rank and file of the Greek Army in the Middle East was tremendous. As the Tsouderos government showed no sign of meeting the PEEA demands, on 30 March a strongly worded memorandum was submitted by a delegation representing the majority of the soldiers, demanding the creation of a government of National Unity with the least possible delay, and stressing the government's responsibilities if this were not done. There is great controversy concerning the instigation of the military ultimatum. It seems by now certain that it did not result from instructions by EAM, as both EAM and PEEA were taken completely by surprise. Whether the British used their agents to provoke it, as has been alleged, or whether, as is more probable, it was a more or less spontaneous reaction on the part of the Republican and left-wing elements who were a majority in the Greek Army, is irrelevant. In any case, it suited British plans admirably. Compelling Tsouderos (who had offered his resignation) to remain in his post, Churchill demanded the categorized rejection of the ultimatum in terms that could only accentuate the crisis. When the first signs of a real mutiny were manifest, the opportunity for purging the Greek Army of all its undesirable elements had arrived.

Accordingly, Churchill went over to open attack. On 9 April he cabled General Paget:

> Our relations are definitely established with the lawfully constituted Greek Government headed by the King .... Neither can Greece find constitutional expression in particular sets of guerrillas, *in many cases indistinguishable from banditti, who are masquerading as the saviours of their country while living on the local villagers.* (Italics supplied).

Only a few months earlier he had referred to the same people as 'gallant guerrillas containing thirty enemy divisions'.

> ... It is a lamentable fact that they [the Greek brigades] should have signalized this opportunity by an undignified, even squalid, exhibition of indiscipline, which many will attribute to an *unworthy fear of being sent to the front.* (Italics supplied).

In fact a permanent source of grievances among the Greek brigade was that they were *not* sent to the front. And

> You will have achieved success if you bring the Brigade under control without bloodshed. But brought under control it must be. (Churchill, vol. 10, p. 195.)

On 14 April he cabled Leeper, British Ambassador to the Greek government-in-exile:

> Do not show yourself over-eager to parley. Simply keep them rounded up by artillery and superior force and let hunger play its part. (p. 197)

and on the next day:

> 'It would be a grave mistake to end this grave business up in a

pleasant kiss all round .... We have to get these men into our hands disarmed, without conditions and, I trust, without bloodshed. (p. 197)

And get them he did. After a series of unsuccessful attempts to find a compromise solution, which were rejected on Churchill's instructions, the mutinous brigades surrendered to the British. Approximately 20,000 men were sent to concentration camps in Libya and Eritrea – almost half the Greek military personnel in the Middle East. The first object of British policy was successfully accomplished. The Greek regular Army was now completely purged and what was left could be counted on to play the Royalist game to the end.

No sooner had the crisis subsided than the demands of PEEA were discussed. Tsouderos was replaced by Sophocles Venizelos. But as, according to Churchill, 'it was not felt that he was suitable for this task', he was replaced by George Papandreou, who was 'specially brought out of Greece' and assumed the premiership on 27 April. The alleged main purpose of the new government was to open negotiations for a coalition government. Thus while the demand for national unity had served as the pretext for the purge of the Greek army, it was also used to entice the political forces of the mainland into a series of complicated discussions, compromises and traps which would eventually undermine the dominant position of the left-wing forces.

Papandreou was the ideal choice for this very subtle and delicate process. A former minister under Eleftherios Venizelos, he was known for his consistent republican feelings; he therefore inspired a maximum of confidence on the left. He had even been offered the presidency of EAM, which he had declined. Now, he was called upon to annihilate EAM. Well educated and highly intelligent, he was the most brilliant orator of his generation. Not least important, he was one of the very few personalities from the old political world who had taken part in the resistance against the Germans and had been imprisoned for it. He also inspired complete confidence in the British. As early as 1942 he had sent a memorandum to Allied HQ explaining the political situation of the country and predicting the necessity of British intervention against the

Communists. Upon assuming the premiership, Papandreou stated his policy with unusual clarity: the aim of his government was to achieve national unity, but without giving in to the Communists at any point. He insisted that the mutineers should be severely punished, and promised the 'suppression of terrorism in the Greek countryside'.

But the obvious trickery did not deter the forces of the left from maintaining their conciliatory attitude. A conference was called in Lebanon for 17 May and representatives of all parties and resistance organizations attended. Papandreou opened the conference with an unprecedentedly fierce attack against EAM and ELAS, whom he described as 'terrorists and murderers'. The murder of Psarros, leader of EKKA, was recent and the EAM/ELAS representatives, who had disavowed it, found themselves on the defensive. The vigour of Papandreou's attack was such that he almost defeated his own purposes, for the conference nearly broke up then and there. But the conciliatory strategy of EAM/ELAS finally prevailed and the conference continued. On 30 May a National Charter was agreed upon and signed. The most important point was the agreement to unify all guerrilla forces of the country and put them under the authority of a national government under Papandreou himself. But the composition of the government, under whose authority the representatives of PEEA and EAM had readily put their military forces, was left open. PEEA had demanded 50 per cent of the portfolios while Papandreou had offered only 25 per cent, and finally outwitted his opponents to such effect that the matter was left undecided.

However, after the return of the representatives of PEEA to Greece, the leadership decided to repudiate the agreement, if Papandreou did not give in to their demands for participation in the government on the basis of a 50–50 ratio. Papandreou played for time, and for three months fruitless proposals and counterproposals were exchanged to no effect. The situation became more and more explosive and by the middle of July the patience of EAM seemed to have been exhausted. Papandreou was accused of breaking the agreement and on 7 July he was called upon immediately to concede half the ministries of EAM and was threatened with the annulment of the Charter if not. The British seemed to be back where they started. But curiously enough EAM policy was to be completely reversed.

Twenty days later, on 29 July, PEEA agreed to enter the government on the single condition that Papandreou should be replaced, and on 15 August even this last demand was abandoned. On 3 September, six representatives of PEEA entered the government in minor and insignificant posts. The *volte-face* was complete.

In order to explain this extraordinary and baffling capitulation of the Left who, by September 1944, had almost total control of Greece, it is necessary to look at the international situation. The British in fact never believed in the possibility of a peaceful solution of the Greek political problem. As early as April 1943 the Chief of the Military Mission in Greece, Colonel Myers, received secret instructions informing him of the political prospects. The opinion stated by the Cairo authorities was that upon liberation, civil war was practically unavoidable. But no such war could be envisaged without Stalin's consent or at least his acquiescence. On 18 May 1944, Eden had a long conversation with the Soviet Ambassador in London, Gusev, concerning the assignment of Rumania and Greece to the Russian and British spheres of influence respectively. The Russians were reluctant and insisted on the agreement of the USA government. After considerable pressure from Churchill, the President gave in and on 19 June Eden informed the Soviet government that this 'general division of responsibility' (Churchill, vol. 11, p. 67) was accepted. This was confirmed by a telegram of Churchill to Stalin dated 11 July. If Stalin's answer was non-committal and did not cover Churchill completely, it was sufficiently reassuring. He was now sure that Stalin would not intervene. On 6 August he wrote to Eden:

> Surely we should tell M. Papandreou he should continue as Prime Minister and defy them all .... We cannot take a man up as we have done Papandreou and let him be thrown to the wolves at the first snarl-

ings of the miserable Greek [Communist] banditti .... The case seems to me to have reached the following point: either we support Papandreou, if necessary with force as we have agreed, or we disinterest ourselves utterly in Greece.

On the same day, he warned his chiefs of staff:

It may be that within a month or so we shall have to put 10,000 or 12,000 men into Athens, with a few tanks, guns, and armoured cars .... Such a force could be embarked now, and would probably be in time for the political crisis, which is of major consequence to the policy of His Majesty's Government. (Churchill, vol. 11, p. 97.)

If the Anglo-Russian agreement on the future of the Balkans produced only slight modifications of British intentions, it led to a complete reversal of Russian policies. On 26 July a Soviet military mission under Colonel Popov was parachuted into Greece and immediately contacted the leadership of the Greek Communist Party. Although the content of the discussions has never been disclosed, it is noteworthy that only three days after the Soviet mission's arrival the first significant shift of EAM's policy took place. It is hardly possible that it was a coincidence. Stalin, it seems, kept to his part of the still informal bargain, and the Greek Communists, who were the decision-making forces of EAM and PEEA, dutifully gave in. Although it is doubtful whether they had been informed of the fact that they had been abandoned for good, there can be no other explanation for their sudden giving in to Papandreou except Soviet pressure. It was only in October, at the Moscow conference between Stalin and Churchill, that the division of the Balkans was 'officially' ratified. On a half sheet of paper the future of the Balkans was rapidly decided upon and Greece was allocated exclusively to Britain. 'Might it not be thought rather cynical if it seemed we had disposed of these issues, so fateful to millions of people, in such an offhand manner? Let us burn the paper,' Churchill suggested after the conclusion of the agreement. 'No, you keep it,' said Stalin (Churchill, vol. 11, p. 201).

Meanwhile, if the political balance had been modified, the military balance inside Greece had remained unchanged. Neither the British nor Papandreou were unaware that the military and political domination of the mainland by EAM was still complete. The hasty arming of collaborationist groups by the Germans did little to close the gap. But the Communists obviously had strict orders from Stalin to comply with British demands up to the end. Having decided on a strategy of a purely political bid for power, they were ready to give in completely on the military level. By the Caserta agreement in September, not only did they agree to be put under the command of the Allied (that is British) military authorities, but also to allow the landing of British troops after the withdrawal of the German forces. ELAS was put under the direct command of General Scobie, who was to lead the British Expeditionary Force. Thus, the fears of Churchill concerning the power gap that would follow the German departure were to a great extent allayed. The British forces could easily provide a political bridgehead, solid enough for the formal assumption of power by the 'recognized' Papandreou government. It is significant that during the Caserta conversations the only objection to this unconditional surrender of the guerrillas was made by the non-Communist General Saraphis, Commander-in-Chief of the ELAS forces, who was obviously not entrusted with the political secrets and, viewing the situation from a professional point of view, justly considered it frightening. However, these objections were easily overruled by the Communist representatives, following the Moscow line. Thus Churchill's intention to 'strike out of the blue without any preliminary crisis', which 'is the best way to forestall the EAM' (Churchill, vol. 11, p. 251) proved unnecessary. Even Churchill himself did not anticipate the extent to which Stalin and consequently the Greek Communist Party was giving him a free hand.

On 12 October 1944 the Germans evacuated Athens. Three days later British troops under General Scobie entered the capital in the midst of demonstrations of indescribable jubilation. The bridgehead had been gained. The power gap in Athens had not lasted for more than a few days. Once again, Churchill's suspicions about a possible bid for power were ill founded. Only a few days before, on 6 October, the official newspaper of the Communist Party published an 'Appeal to the Greek People' on the occasion of the liberation, ending with the words:

> You will now become the goldsmiths of public order and of democratic liberties. Patriots, all united to complete, together with ELAS and *our Allies*, the Greek liberation, *under the leadership of a government of National Unity*. (Italics supplied.)

It is thus obvious that Communist strategy was still strictly legalistic. When Papandreou arrived at the head of the Government on 18 October, jubilation reached its peak. But if the government's authority was at first sight generally recognized, the situation was far from simple. Real power was still held by EAM, whose forces reigned unchallenged all over the country. The effective authority of Papandreou was restricted to the Athens region and a handful of other towns where the British Army had acquired a foothold.

The transfer of power from the guerrillas to the central government was the main preoccupation of both the British and Papandreou. As Churchill puts it: 'The testing time for our arrangements had now come. At the Moscow conference I had obtained Russian abstention at a heavy price.' Under the terms of the Caserta agreement all guerrilla bands were to be disbanded and, together with the small Greek forces from the Middle East, were to form the nucleus of the new Greek Army under the national government's authority. Very soon, however, insuperable divergences of opinion between the British and the Communists emerged over this crucial issue. The respective numbers of the forces to enter the Army, the question of whether the units to be formed should retain their distinct character or should be integrated, the problem of the new Army's leadership, were matters it proved impossible to agree upon.

The most crucial issue was the future of the heavily armed Middle East Brigade, which, after the purge, was fanatically Royalist. EAM insisted on its disbandment on an equal basis with the guerrilla forces, whereas Papandreou refused to accept this. On 27 November discussions were suddenly broken off. Papandreou and EAM accused one another of breaking promises, and the deadlock was complete. It is impossible to extract the truth from the accusations that were subsequently made. It seems, however, that a compromise agreement had been reached and countersigned by both Papandreou and the Communists. Next day (28 November) the Communists cancelled the agreement, accusing Papandreou of duplicity. How and why the fateful decision was taken is still unknown.

In view of the overall strategy of the Communist Party in the past and again in the future, the sudden toughness is hard to explain. Be this as it may, the vital decision to engage in armed struggle if a satisfactory compromise should prove impossible seems to have been reached that same night.

Whether or not Churchill actually believed in an inevitable attempt at a Communist take-over, he most certainly had prepared his own plans for military intervention. On 7 November he had cabled Eden:

> In my opinion, having paid the price we have to Russia for freedom of action in Greece, we should not hesitate to use British troops to support ... Papandreou. ... This implies that British troops should certainly intervene to check acts of lawlessness .... I hope the Greek Brigade will soon arrive, and will not hesitate to shoot if necessary. ... *I fully expect a clash with EAM and we must not shrink from it, provided the ground is well chosen.* (Churchill, vol. 11, p. 254; italics supplied.)

With the backing of the British and after consulting Ambassador Leeper, without whom, according to Woodhouse (op. cit., 106), he did not make a single move, Papandreou decided to take a harder line: he summoned the cabinet and issued a formal order that all guerrillas should be disbanded by 10 December. On 1 December the crisis was further accentuated. General Scobie took it upon himself to repeat the government's decision in terms of an ultimatum. The atmosphere had been rapidly deteriorating as a result of the activities of the extreme right-wing collaborationist groups, which had been formed by the Germans in 1943 to fight EAM. Mainly composed of members of the security services of the Metaxas dictatorship, these 'Security Battalions' were well armed and had been used against the resistance. Some other anti-Communist groups, and in particular General Zervas, leader of EDES and of other groups of minor importance in Macedonia and the Athens district, had openly collaborated with the Security battalions against the EAM. Four-cornered situations had developed, in which genuine resistance fighters aligned themselves with the collaborationists against the Communists while continuing to fight the occupation forces. After the liberation it was inevitable that old feuds should be re-opened and accounts settled.

The future of the collaborators had not hitherto been an object of disagreement. All parties had agreed in principle that they should be severely punished. In fact the members of the collaborationist governments and a number of the most notorious German agents were arrested by the government immediately after liberation. But the great bulk of them were hiding, waiting for events. As it became gradually clear that the differences between EAM on the one hand and Papandreou and the British on the other were seriously aggravated, a double process was started off. On the one hand the attempted reorganization of the police and the gendarmerie on the government's side was taking the form of open recruitment of collaborationists, who, having found a new nest, were only too glad to prove their attachment to their new masters, by exceeding their orders and terrorizing their opponents when they had the opportunity. On the other hand, a large number of ELAS groups, who were still in control of the countryside and feared that the collaborationists would ultimately escape their well-deserved punishment and function as an armed force against them – as in fact the majority who did escape or were given over by the ELAS to the regular authorities did – took it upon themselves to organize popular courts which, by October, were functioning all over the country. Naturally enough, the procedure was often summary and many hundreds of persons were condemned to death and executed. This in turn led to attempts to reorganize the fascist bands, which also resulted in a number of terrorist raids by EAM against the strongholds of reorganized collaborators. The grievances of the civil wars that had been fought between the resistance organizations were revived and the remnants of the right-wing guerrillas took the side of the Security Battalions.

This more or less spontaneous regrouping of the forces of the extreme right was immediately encouraged and soon even officially sponsored by the British. Despite the clause in the Caserta agreement according to which the Security Battalions were considered as enemy formations and were to be treated accordingly, on 27 September, before the German withdrawal, General Scobie issued an order to General Shiliotopoulos, who had been appointed Military Commander of Athens, to the effect that 'after the departure of the Germans, the Security Battalions should receive instructions to *desert and hide*, or else to give themselves up to the British.' And by the middle of November, 'Arrangements were made to raise and equip National Guard battalions, each 500 strong. Ultimately there were thirty of these; they proved very useful in rounding up armed hostile civilians and guarding areas cleared by our own troops' (Churchill, vol. 11, p. 254).

In this atmosphere, the order issued by Scobie to disband ELAS provoked the final crisis. The EAM ministers resigned from the National Unity government and a mass demonstration was called for 3 December. Permission for the rally had been given by Papandreou. But, under the pressure of Leeper, he then decided to forbid it. However, the demonstration was not cancelled, and on 3 December large crowds assembled in Constitution Square. Unarmed and unsuspecting, they shouted anti-Papandreou but, on the whole, not anti-British slogans. Suddenly out of the blue there was firing and hundreds of dead and wounded covered the pavement. The fighting had begun.

There was much controversy about who did the shooting. It is now beyond doubt that it was the police who fired in cold blood and without any provocation. The police chief admitted it, claiming 'self-defence'. An eye-witness, the British Officer, Byford-Jones, states that he himself saw and heard the orders to shoot on the unsuspecting crowd. Similarly, *The Times*, United Press and New York radio correspondents are unanimous that the shooting was deliberate and unprovoked. It was only later, when anti-Communist hysteria became general, that any doubt was cast on the cause of 'Bloody Sunday'. What still remains unclear, however, is who gave the orders. Whether they came from the Greek government or the British authorities, or whether they resulted from a plot of ultra-rightists who wanted to precipitate events, is not yet proven.

Some commentators consider that the massacre did not provoke the conflict but only precipitated it. This raises a more fundamental question. There can be no doubt that EAM did not originally desire an armed seizure of power. Even if one disregards the effects of Russian advice, it is absurd to believe, in the light of all official and unofficial evidence, that the Communists intended to make a bid for power. If this had been their aim, there can be no explanation for their successive retreats, both political and military. The example of Tito, who not only refused to accept any authority other than the popular government he himself controlled, but specifically warned Churchill against any attempt at British military intervention in Yugoslavia (which finally deterred the British from intervening even though they had agreed on a 50–50 basis of influence with Stalin) is telling indeed. Had the Communist Party opted for armed struggle, it was scarcely likely to wait until December 1944.

The fact that the Greek Communists had continually been in touch with Tito during the occupation only makes their differences in strategy more pronounced. As early as August 1943 the secretary of the Communist Party, Siantos, had assured the British that 'Greece belongs to a region of Europe where the British assume all responsibilities'. This extraordinary declaration was made to appease British fears arising from a recent conference between Greek and Yugoslav guerrilla leaders. Any 'subordination to a pan-Balkan guerrilla movement was therefore out of the question' (Siantos). Co-ordination between the two national liberation movements was restricted to intelligence and tactical considerations. Siantos's assurances seem to have represented EAM's true intentions. S. Voukmanovic (Tempo), who had been Tito's liaison officer with the ELAS, later accused the ELAS leaders of being 'ideologically unprepared to take over power' and stressed the *legalistic* attitude of the Greek Communist Party in contrast to the Yugoslav one. Even if their attitude could not have been different in the beginning, in view of their expectation that a full-scale Anglo-American attack was about to be launched through the Balkans, the Teheran conference dissipated all such considerations. Nevertheless, at no moment did EAM change its policy. Indeed, it softened its position considerably after the pressure of the Soviet military mission. Since the Communists relinquished their military supremacy and did their utmost to achieve a political solution which would have enabled them to continue the struggle on a parliamentary basis, it is absurd to believe in an organized and planned Communist aggression. Finally, it should be noted that, in the fateful days when fighting started in Athens, the great bulk of the ELAS troops were stationed at great distances from the capital. The problem for the Communists had been how to avoid unilateral disarmament, not how to fight.

CHAPTER 6

December 1944. The Turning Point (1944–6)

THE twenty-eight dead and over a hundred wounded of 3 December marked the beginning of armed confrontation. EAM called a general strike and a mass meeting for 4 December. The rally was held without any incidents caused by either EAM or the British. But while the demonstrators were dispersing they were attacked by armed groups of the ultra-right organization 'X' (led by Colonel Grivas) and other collaborationist bands. These attacks resulted in over a hundred deaths. Although probably neither the government nor the British were responsible, this was the last straw. On the same evening, armed attacks by ELAS against the still unpurged police stations began and Scobie proclaimed martial law, calling on ELAS to evacuate Athens within two days.

Next day (5 December), Scobie's action was confirmed with formal orders from Churchill:

> I have given instructions to General Wilson to make sure that all forces are left with you and all possible reinforcements are sent to you.... Do not hesitate to fire at any armed male in Athens who assails the British authority or Greek authority with which we are working. It would be well, of course, if your command were reinforced by the authority of some [sic] Greek government, and Papandreou is being told by Leeper to stop and help. *Do not hesitate to act as if you were in a conquered city where a local rebellion is in progress.*
>
> With regard to the ELAS bands approaching from the outside, you should surely be able with your armour to give some of these a lesson which will make others unlikely to try.... *We have to hold and dominate Athens. It would be a great thing to succeed in this without bloodshed if possible, but also with bloodshed if necessary.* (Churchill, vol. 11, p. 256; italics in original)

Although Scobie was militarily unprepared for a full-scale battle, as he did not have more than 10,000 men at his immediate disposal out of 26,500 British troops in the whole of

Greece, Churchill's decision was to proceed immediately to a final confrontation. His disregard for indigenous political elements can only be understood in the light of his overall decision that Greece was to be kept, at all costs, within the British orbit of 'responsibility'. As he characteristically cabled Leeper on the same day (5 December):

> This is no time to dabble in Greek politics or to imagine that Greek politicians of various shades can affect the situation. *You should not worry about Greek government compositions*. The matter is one of life or death.
>
> You must urge Papandreou to stand to his duty, and assure him he will be supported by all our forces if he does so. The day has long gone past when any particular group of Greek politicians can influence this mob rising. His only chance is to come through with us. (Churchill, vol. 11, p. 257; italics supplied)

On this last point, Churchill proved most definitely right. Papandreou, who had offered his resignation, revoked it and until the end of the war he unquestioningly complied with Leeper's instructions.

But if British policy was clear enough, the aims and intentions of the Communist Party and EAM were still self-contradictory. Although the decision to launch an armed struggle was reached on 27 November, as we have seen, armed action was still considered subsidiary to a political solution. Even after 4 December, when fighting had begun, there were serious disagreements about the extent it should take and about the more general strategy it should be integrated in. For not only did a considerable fraction of EAM still believe in the possibility of a compromise solution; it also hesitated as to whether or not the struggle should be undertaken with all its forces. In the first few days the ELAS fighters received specific orders to avoid any battles against British forces and to confine themselves to fighting against the Greek Royalist troops and the police. Even later on, when the possibility of keeping the British outside the struggle was obviously not envisaged any more, the ELAS forces showed great reluctance to shoot at the British. Thus during the whole war the British lost only 237 men, an absurdly low number if one considers the length and tenacity of the battles. It is also significant that the British garrisons in Salonica and the other towns where they were stationed were never attacked, despite the enormous superiority in men and materials of ELAS everywhere except in Athens. Another paradox, only to be explained if one accepts that the Communists never ceased to believe in a political solution, is that during the war in Athens very few attempts were made to reinforce the units engaged in desperate fighting with other ELAS troops stationed elsewhere. Instead of sending all available forces to Athens, the ELAS leadership launched an attack against the remaining forces of EDES in Epirus which, however, had already started to demobilize. EDES was rapidly dissolved, thereby ensuring an ELAS monopoly of military and political power in the whole of rural Greece at the very time when the forces of ELAS in Athens were confronted with growing difficulties. While slightly superior to the British in numbers (they have been estimated at 20,000) they were seriously lacking in equipment, training and supplies.

Nevertheless, the first days brought considerable success to ELAS, who confined the British into a small area not more than a mile square, in the centre of the town, including Colonaki, the Athenian Belgravia. Instead of launching a final attack against the British positions, which could have resulted in the elimination of the bridgehead, ELAS dispersed their efforts in peripheral objectives in order to eliminate the pockets of Royalist-controlled areas. This indecision over an all-out attack should be considered in the light of the repeated attempts to achieve an armistice, even at the time when their military position was still quite challenging. Thus on 10 December representatives of EAM/ELAS visited Scobie and asked for an armistice. But Scobie, who had his instructions, proposed terms amounting to unconditional surrender: ELAS should immediately evacuate Attica and surrender their arms. Five days later new conciliatory proposals were met with the same rigidity. Churchill was adamant. Feeling absolutely secure with respect to Stalin's attitude, he decided to break ELAS, which he described as Trotskyist in the House of Commons– a wink to Stalin – and to accept nothing except utter submission. On 8 December he told Scobie:

> There is much talk in the press tonight of a peace offer by ELAS. Naturally we should be glad to have this matter settled, but you should make quite sure, so far as your influence goes, that we do not give away for the sake of kindness what has been won or can still be won by our troops. It would seem that anything less satisfactory than the terms agreed upon before the revolt took place should not be accepted. . . .
>
> *The clear objective is the defeat of the EAM. The ending of the fighting is subsidiary to this.* (Churchill, vol. 11, p. 258; Italics supplied)

Although international and British public opinion was greatly aroused (on 13 December the Trades Union Congress expressed with an astounding majority – 2,455,000 votes against 137,000 – its regret at the policy of the British Government in Greece) and it was obvious that faulty intelligence had led to a miscalculation of ELAS power, the resolution of Churchill was undaunted. Field-Marshal Alexander, who had replaced Wilson as Commander-in-Chief of the Middle East forces, kept men and supplies pouring in to Athens and by the 20 December the balance of forces favoured the British. The military position of Scobie being secure, the problem became how to achieve a political solution. On 22 December Churchill cabled Alexander:

> There is no question of embarking in any military operations away from the Athens–Piraeus area. We must however have a military foundation there on which a Greek Government of some kind or other can function. . . .
>
> Thereafter we do not intend to stay in Greece except for such reasonable period as may be necessary to let the new Government, whatever it is, gain for itself a National Army or Militia, in the hope that these may be able to conduct elections, plebiscites, etc. [!] We can achieve no political solution while negotiating from a base of weakness and frustration. (Churchill, vol. 11, p. 274)

On Christmas Day Churchill visited Athens to take a look for himself. A conference was called with representatives of all the Greek political parties, EAM, the British authorities, and curiously enough Colonel Popov of the Soviet military mission, who throughout the hostilities had been quietly staying in full uniform in the Grande Bretagne hotel on Constitution Square, which also housed the military headquarters of Scobie. Churchill himself paid tribute to Stalin's good faith:

Stalin adhered strictly and faithfully to our agreement of October and in all the long weeks of fighting the Communists in the streets of Athens not one word of reproach came from Pravda or Izvestia. (Churchill, vol. 11.)

But it was the turn of the representations of EAM/ELAS to be adamant. Still believing in the possibility of a political victory, despite the fact that their military position had taken a turn for the worse, they presented a series of impossible demands. Not only did they return to their demand for 50 per cent of the seats in government, including the Ministry of the Interior and other key ministries; they also demanded the dissolution of the regular Greek Brigades, the purge of the police forces and general elections before April. The demands were naturally rejected and the fighting resumed. By the beginning of January ELAS's military position had become untenable and on 5 January Athens was evacuated.

It is difficult to explain this second sudden hardening of the Communists' position. They must have realized that their military position had been seriously impaired. Continuous reinforcements had given Scobie an undoubted supremacy. The control of the airport enabled the British to keep adding to their fighting troops until they finally reached 40,000 men. On the other hand no serious reinforcement of ELAS forces was being attempted. The bulk of their forces were still tied up in the dispersal and elimination of the minor bands in the countryside. No general offensive against the British was envisaged, nor was any such operation now feasible. It seems that EAM grossly overestimated the impact of domestic and international protest against Churchill's policy. They probably interpreted his presence in Athens as a sign of weakness, rather than style, and tried to make the best out of their opponents' presumed need to give in. Perhaps they also believed in some kind of diplomatic support from the Soviet Union. In this they were to be rudely disappointed. On the very next day, while the battles had been resumed, the Papandreou government was officially recognized by Stalin, who also nominated Ambassador Sergeiev to Athens. The motives behind these fatal miscalculations of the situation are still an object of speculation. It has been implied that it was Tito's influence that moved the Greek Communist Party towards the hardening of their position, though such an interpretation is not corroborated. It has also been said that we should find the clue in Soviet encouragement, in view of the well-known docility of the KKE to Stalin's desires. But all official and unofficial evidence shows that, at least at that stage, Stalin's attitude was discouraging. In reality the strategy of the KKE during those fateful days has yet to be brought to light. The responsibility for the inexplicable mistakes, vacillations and hesitations cannot be settled by pointing out the undoubted inadequacy of the Communist leadership. The real decision-making processes in the Greek Communist movement will only be illuminated if and when the Communist leaders in exile decide that the time has come to write their history.

Other events with even more far-reaching repercussions were taking place by the end of the month. While the military situation was gradually worsening, the ELAS troops not only intensified their punitive measures against the collaborationist and fascist bands, but started to arrest civilian hostages, whom they hurried out of Athens and into the mountains. This measure was to constitute one of the main and most effective propaganda instruments in the hands of the future right-wing governments. It was also of fundamental importance in the gradual switching of popular allegiance from left to right. It is impossible to estimate with certainty the extent of this brutal practice. Figures have been given ranging from 15,000 to 35,000 from the Athens district alone. Out of these it seems that approximately 4,000 were executed or died as a result of bad conditions. It should, however, be pointed out that these malpractices were not confined to the Communist side. During December and January the Greek and British authorities arrested almost 15,000 people in the Athens area alone. Most of them were deported to concentration camps in North

Africa and many of them never returned. More than military defeat, the atrocities committed during the last days of December were to lead to the tragedy that was to befall not only the Communists but the progressive forces in general.

Having secured their military bridgehead, the British turned to settling the political problem. This involved the form of the regime and the composition of the government. The King had given in to Churchill's pressure against an immediate return and agreed to the appointment of a Regent. On 1 January 1945 Archbishop Damaskinos accepted the Regency and proclaimed the need to end the fighting. Papandreou had by now served his purpose. He had been exposed by the political intrigues that led to the Communists' defeat. A fresh personality, able to act as a conciliator but malleable enough to serve British plans, was needed. General Nicholas Plastiras, an honest but irresolute veteran with the aura of the anti-Royalist and uncompromisingly Republican revolution of 1922 which he had led, met with both these requirements. He had been flown into Athens some weeks before after a ten-year exile in France, during which he had lost contact with new political realities. He had also been talked into swearing allegiance to the King, a fact that was not disclosed by the British until he was needed no more. His appointment was therefore accepted by the Communists as a conciliatory sign and an armistice was signed on 11 January.

The armistice marked the end of the war. But the country was in ruins. The degree of destruction Greece had suffered can only be compared with that in Yugoslavia, Poland and Russia. From 1940 to 1944 550,000 people (8 per cent of the population) had perished, and 34 per cent of the total national wealth had been destroyed; 401,500 houses were completely destroyed, leaving 1,200,000 people homeless; 1,770 villages had been totally burnt down; the large harbours, railway tracks, steam engines, telephone networks, civil airports and bridges had been completely destroyed; 73 per cent of cargo ship tonnage, 94 per cent of passenger ships had been sunk; 56 per cent of the roads were destroyed, 65 per cent of private cars, 60 per cent of trucks and 80 per cent of buses;

60 per cent of the horses, 60 per cent of the cattle and 80 per cent of small animals had died; 25 per cent of the forests had been burnt; in 1944 cereal production was down by 40 per cent, tobacco production by 89 per cent and currant production by 66 per cent.

The Varkiza Agreement signed on 12 February between the EAM, the British and the Plastiras government was the product of long and strenuous negotiations. All guerrilla units were to be disbanded and ELAS was to surrender its arms within two weeks, while EAM would not be represented in the government, which undertook to hold a plebiscite on the question of the monarchy, within the year. On the other hand, the Communist Party was allowed to continue its political activities and an amnesty was given to ELAS and EAM fighters. This clause was the main object of disagreement. The amnesty did not include offences under common criminal law, an omission which proved to be fatal. Whereas the leaders of EAM were safe from sanctions, the rank and file of the guerrillas were subject to unrestricted persecution. For by stretching the law there was hardly any guerrilla activity that could not be brought under some common-law offence. Tens of thousands of resistance fighters were to suffer as the result of this castrated armistice, while the leaders, whose activities were by definition political, were left untouched. Their complete capitulation at a time when, while beaten in Athens, they still controlled the greatest part of Greece created the 'legal' background to the white terror which was to follow and eventually paved the way to the civil war. Once more Soviet pressure seems to contribute to the explanation. Partsalides, a member of the Politburo of the KKE, openly alluded to external pressures when he was later accused of capitulation. It should be remembered that the Varkiza Agreement coincides in time with Yalta. Stalin may have been in a hurry to prove his good faith.

The Varkiza Agreement was by and large fulfilled on the Communists' part. 100 guns, 81 mortars, 419 machine guns, 2,115 automatic rifles, 138 individual mortars, 48,653 rifles and revolvers and 57 anti-tank rifles (a greater number than had been agreed upon) were duly surrendered to the authorities. A considerable amount of weapons and ammunition was, however, not surrendered. It does not seem that the withholding of the guns was due to a decision of the Communist leaders to retain them for another armed struggle. But a number of ELAS groups, including the redoubtable guerilla fighter Aris Velouchiotis, refused to accept the Varkiza Agreement and took once more to the mountains. As the white terror developed, more and more ELAS fighters refused to surrender their arms. But they were immediately disowned by the Communist Party and EAM, who had issued orders that all guerrillas should disarm quietly and rapidly. Aris himself was to be caught and killed, but in spite of this his example was followed by many of his companions who stayed in the mountains in order to escape arrest and execution.

By the middle of 1945 the white terror had reached enormous dimensions. A memorandum was signed on 5 June by Plastiras (who by now had served his purpose too, and had been replaced), and by Sophoulis, Kafandaris, Mylonas and Tsouderos, leaders of the Centre parties that had begun to revive. It stated:

> The terror initiated by the extreme right in the whole country after the December incidents is being amplified every day. Its development and its extension render the life of all non-royalist citizens impossible and exclude the hope that we can proceed to a free plebiscite or to elections. The terrorist organizations of the extreme right, which had been armed by the Germans and had collaborated with them, have not been disarmed or prosecuted, but have allied themselves to the security forces in order to strangle completely all democratic thought.

In fact the right-wing extremists constituted the bulk of the security forces themselves, which, far from being purged, had been enriched with the members of organizations that up to that point had functioned on a 'private' basis. The then Under-Secretary of War later admitted that 'the First National Guard Battalions were formed with members of the Security Battalions, on my own initiative.' Simultaneously with the official security forces and in full collaboration with them, Grivas's 'X' organization, which later claimed to have reached 200,000 members, had as its main object the persecution and murder of the ex-guerrillas of ELAS. In the short period from February to July 1945 20,000 persons had been arrested, over 500 murdered and 2,961 condemned to death. (The latter figure was announced by the Greek government.) In December 1945 the Minister of Justice declared:

> ... the number of imprisoned persons is 17,984. Of these 2,388 have been legally condemned and 15,596 are detained preventively.... 48,956 are being prosecuted for their activities as EAM/ELAS members. The total number of persons to be charged, including those already detained is, according to our estimate, over 80,000.

According to EAM, from Varkiza till the election of 31 March 1946, 1,289 persons were murdered, 6,671 were badly wounded, 31,632 were tortured and 84,931 were arrested.

Meanwhile, in February, the Yalta conference had taken place. As far as the Balkan issues were concerned it only ratified the previous agreements between Churchill and Stalin. But its international implications were far-reaching, in as much as the spheres of influence in the Balkans were definitely agreed upon whereas the previous agreements had an allegedly provisional character. As Isaac Deutcher has pointed out, Stalin was in a bizarre, Byzantine way legalistically scrupulous in his bargains with his bourgeois allies. It is the tragedy of the Greek Communists that they never realized this. Unlike the French and Italian Communists who (especially the latter) had to confront similar, if not so serious, provocations from the extreme right after the end of the war, the Greek Communist Party's attitude was short-sighted. One has only to recall Togliatti's calls for moderation and non-retaliation when an attempt on his life had just failed. By contrast, persecution gradually led the Greek Communist movement to a revolutionary attitude.

In June 1945 Zachariades, the Moscow-trained Secretary-General of the Greek Communist Party, who, after having spent three years in Metaxas's gaols, had been transferred to Germany and interned in a concentration camp where he miraculously escaped with his life, returned to Greece and immediately assumed his old post. In the beginning he pursued a line fully recognizing British supremacy in Greece and ratified the decision to demobilize and terminate the armed struggle. But this readjustment of Communist strategy was not accompanied by a broader re-evaluation of the situation. The main consideration of Zachariades was obedience to Soviet wishes. His servility towards Stalin and his refusal to support the national territorial claims in northern Epirus (now part of Albania) helped to reinforce the propaganda against the Communists. He accepted the integration of Greece within the Western bloc, which he formulated as 'the Greek axis, uniting the British-Mediterranean with the Balkan-European (Russian) poles', but only so long as it was dictated by Stalin.

Thus, for the time being, Communist hopes seemed to be founded on the social turmoil that would inevitably arise from the sad economic situation of the country. A galloping inflation that had resulted from the total collapse of the economy during the occupation could not be controlled, and for all the efforts of the United Nations Relief organization (UNRRA), not only was the reconstruction programme of no effect but even food was badly lacking in the provinces. The puppet governments that had succeeded Plastiras were corrupt, incompetent and had only nominal authority, and the country was plunged into renewed chaos.

Real power was still held by the British Army, and Scobie, together with British Ambassador Leeper, imposed both governments and policies. Between January 1945 and April 1946 eight governments were formed, the longest of these being headed by Admiral Voulgaris, who had played an important role in the suppression of the 1944 Middle East Army mutiny. The advent of the Labour Government in 1945 did not change British policy in the least. Whenever Greek governments tried to prevent the takeover of the Army and the security services by the ultra-Royalist clique, they were confronted by the veto of the British Military Mission. Moreover, a permanent Economic Mission was installed, acting as an independent Ministry of Economic Affairs, organizing the activities of the relief funds and even responsible for issuing the currency. Economic difficulties were in fact exacerbated by the rigidity of British economic control. All important decisions had to pass through London, so much so that one of the major demands of Premier Tsaldaris when he visited London in July 1946 was that the British Ambassador or Mission Commander be authorized to take decisions on the spot on matters of armament, equipment, rations and uniforms.

The pre-war economic influence of Britain was also strengthened. The Athens–Piraeus tramways and trains, the water company, the electric power company, were restored to the British, who had built and operated them before the war.

Elections were planned for March 1946. The growing terrorism made electoral campaigning difficult if not impossible for anyone but the Right. Not only the Communists but also the Centre parties, heirs of the pre-war Liberals, denounced the electoral farce that was to take place. Foreign Minister Sophianopoulas resigned in January and Vice-Premier Kafandaris in March, followed by twelve other members of the government. They all demanded postponement of the elections until a minimum of normality could be obtained. Nevertheless, British Foreign Secretary Bevin flatly refused Premier Sophoulis's demand for postponement of the elections, and the latter remained fixed for 31 March. Thereupon the Communists and a large section of the Republicans (Centrists) committed one more fateful mistake. They decided to abstain and thereby deprived Greek democratic forces of parliamentary representation over the next four crucial years. For, despite the white terror, they stood a good chance of at least imposing their presence on the new political world that was about to be created. Their abstention suited Bevin's policy admirably. When, two days after the deadline for the nomination of candidates, a considerable fraction of the Left decided to reconsider and asked for an extended deadline, Bevin again exercised his veto on Sophoulis. One half of the Greek population would thus not be represented in Parliament. Extraparliamentary opposition would become the only kind of opposition. And the Communist Party would be dragged once more by its leaders to the only path towards power which abstention from the elections had left open: civil war.

The main issue in the elections was the monarchy. The parties of the pre-Metaxas period had managed to reconstruct themselves out of their scattered remnants. The Populists, under Constantine Tsaldaris, espoused the royal cause and with some 600,000 votes won an absolute majority. The total number of votes barely exceeded 1,100,000 out of 2.2 millions on the electoral roll. The abstentions were thus close to 50 per cent. If one takes into consideration that a large number of EAM supporters had not been put on the register, the extended multiple voting practised by the Rightists who were in control of the state machine, and the climate of open terrorism that reigned, the discrepancy between elected Parliament and public opinion becomes even more manifest. But regardless of whether the people were represented, the elections had the important effect of legitimizing the government and consolidating the Royalist revival. The plebiscite on the question of the monarchy, held in September, brought the expected result: King George's return was secured by a 68.9 per cent majority and the King immediately returned to Greece.

Thus British policy had met with complete success. While the British found their military allies in the extreme Right and collaborationist groups, who they had carefully preserved, armed and used against the ELAS, the political allies were sought among the progressive and Republican pre-war political circles, who would be able to pose as conciliators and moderates. Papandreou, Plastiras and Sophoulis were successively called upon to play this role. The King, whose presence could have only been interpreted as a sanctioning of right-wing supremacy, was carefully kept away. The governments were encouraged to talk in terms of a conciliatory line, while the building up of the Army and security forces was entrusted to more unscrupulous hands. The double structure of power, democratic in the political façade but Royalist-fascist in the forces of coercion, which was gradually built up from 1943, was to be a crucial factor in the future. For the construction of the new Army as an autonomous entity, not subject to governmental authority, did not end with the termination of the civil war. Despite the fact that the right wing was in power between 1952 and 1963, the army remained 'untouchable'. Under the nominal authority of the King, the special status of the armed forces which was planned by the British in 1944–6 became the dominating characteristic in the Greek political game.

But the extent of the now institutionalized white terror was such that it almost defeated its own purposes. By March 1946 the arrests had reached 85,000 and the 'X' gangs were raiding the provinces in quest of more victims. The new Tsaldaris government did nothing to control the situation. The collaborators were unofficially, if not officially, rehabilitated. Legislation passed by the Quisling governments was retrospectively ratified. No restraint was imposed on the Right extremists, who continued their activities unperturbed.

The revival of the Quislings is vividly illustrated in the Twentieth Century Fund *Report on the Greeks* (1947). 'Notorious wealthy collaborators – industrialists and others – received protection, patronage and contracts from the government' (p. 35). UNRRA supplies were sold to these businessmen, who resold them at huge profits. Instability further provided opportunities for speculation: 'Industrialists and businessmen ... hate to put their money into enterprise unless it promises at least 40 per cent profit on the investment, because they could make that much simply by manipulating their money in foreign exchange' (p. 75). It is estimated that a thousand families (a half of one per cent of the population) enjoyed over a half of the total private revenue (Mathiopoulos, *Geschichte der Sozialen Frage in Griechenland*, p. 164)! Paul Porter, the American in charge of relief at the time, writes: 'Profiteers, that is traders, speculators, and black marketeers, thrive in wealth and luxury, a problem with which no government has effectively dealt. At the same time masses of people live on a bare subsistence level' (*Economic Report*, April 1947).

One such specific case puts the matter in better perspective. Mr Tsironikos was Vice-President of the Quisling government throughout the occupation. He was also a personal friend of King George, whom he had met in the twenties in Bucharest, where the King was spending his exile, and where Tsironikos represented British interests in petroleum. He had come to Greece for the first time a few days before the outbreak of the Second World War. When the Germans overran the country Tsironikos was immediately appointed No. 2 in the Quisling government and put in charge of economic affairs, where he remained to the end of the occupation. Upon the Germans' retreat from Greece he was one of the few personalities who followed them. Arrested by the Americans when Germany collapsed, he was transferred to Greece, where he was condemned to death as a collaborator and was, of course, not executed. After a short stay in the then Security Headquarters, under luxurious conditions, he was a free man. By 1952, when Marshall Papagos's government came to power, the process of rehabilitation was complete: Tsironikos was appointed Special Counsellor to the Minister of Coordination, Spiridon Markezinis. The latter had been Private Secretary to King George in the Middle East and had been entrusted with the economic organization of the 1946 referendum on the monarchy, for which he had been given *carte blanche*. In 1952 Markezinis was the rising star of the right wing and was considered an economic wizard. Tsironikos was dispatched to Bonn to organize Markezinis's official visit to the Federal German capital, aimed to re-establish the economic links between Greece and the Bundesrepublik. One year later, the Siemens-Telefunken scandal broke out: a letter of Markezinis's was made public, in which he promised Ludwig Erhard, then Minister of Economic Affairs, to turn over the Greek broadcasting system to Telefunken and the nationalized telephone company to Siemens. It is all as if the invisible nexus of Greek and foreign capitalist interests which operated before the war had continued to function despite the war and had eventually remerged intact once the immediate post-war turmoil settled down.

The disarray of the Communist Party had been naturally intensified. Despite the Party line, the number of ex-guerrilla fighters who took to the mountains was constantly growing. They soon organized themselves into 'self-defence units' and sporadic fighting in the mountains became more frequent. Further, thousands of former guerrillas crossed the frontier to Yugoslavia, Bulgaria or Albania. Even so, the leadership of the Communist Party hesitated on the course it should follow. Although the idea of a nation-wide guerrilla war had been implicit at their Seventh Party Congress in September 1945, the decision was not reached until February 1946, when it had become clear that the general elections would be stage-managed.

The internal evolution alone does not suffice to explain the switch in Communist policy. Although there is no evidence that the Soviets actually encouraged the new insurrection, it should be pointed out that by the middle of 1945 the Soviet's attitude had also hardened. During the Potsdam conference, Molotov presented a memorandum to the British in which he stated for the first time that the Soviet Union disagreed with and protested against the way Britain was handling the Greek problem 'on the grounds of an old and indefinite authorization'. Stalin further demanded a military base in Greece for the Soviet Union and specified either Salonica or Alexandroupolis, a demand to which Churchill was to give publicity.

The Seventh Communist Party Congress, during which the possibility of insurrection was put forward for the first time, followed a few weeks after Potsdam. But the situation remained unclear for another six months. Not until January 1946, at the first meeting of the United Nations Security Council, did the Soviet government demand the immediate withdrawal of British troops from Greece, while the final decision to launch an armed struggle was reached in February. But already in December 1945 members of the Communist Party central committee had met with representatives of the Yugoslav and Bulgarian general staffs in Petrich, Bulgaria. The actual discussions have not been disclosed, but they must have referred to the feasibility of the venture as well as to the military help which the Yugoslavs and Bulgarians were prepared to offer. To what extent aid was offered, whether or not the Soviet Union openly encouraged the Greek Communist Party to take up arms, whether Stalin really believed in the possibility of a Communist take-over or only desired to intensify tension in the Balkans to which he sacrificed the Greek Communists, are questions that cannot yet be answered. But it appears to be beyond any reasonable doubt that Soviet influence was as important for the resumption of armed struggle in 1946 as it has been for the softening of the Communist position in the middle of 1944. Once more the intransigence of the Greek reactionaires worked hand in hand with Soviet influence, this time leading to a civil war which was to last for three years.

However, the Greek Communist Party's policy was still vacillating and at the national conference of the Party that was held in April 1946 the subject was not even touched. Even as late as August 1946, when General Marcos Vafiadis was given the task of building up the 'Democratic Army' in the mountains, the Communists still hoped to be able to avoid an armed confrontation, and until July 1947, when full-scale civil war had already begun, significant efforts were directed towards convincing the Centrists to exercise pressure inside the government for the normalization of the situation. But once more, the Communists overestimated their bargaining power. Encouraged by some early successes in the field, and tragically uninformed about British and American intentions, they put forward a series of demands which, under the circumstances, can only be considered as exorbitant. The Royalist government, recently endorsed by a plebiscite and general elections, and enjoying military, material and moral support from both the British and the American governments, was backed by an army which was rapidly reorganizing itself into a far from negligible fighting force. They could not accept discussion on a basis of equality. Repeated proposals were rejected one after the other. Greece was heading towards total civil war that was to have immeasurable repercussions on her future. Once more, the die was cast.

CHAPTER 7

Civil War (1946–9)

THE decision of the Communist Party to launch a new armed struggle was based, whatever else may be said about it, on a fundamental error in the evaluation of the balance of forces. Though economically ruined, unable to start on reconstruction without a continuous flow of foreign aid, and with a government that did not represent popular feeling, Greece in 1946 was nevertheless in a different situation from that of two years before. The Communists now stood alone. Most of the small parties that had cooperated with the KKE in the framework of EAM had by now abandoned the Communists. The relative stabilization of the internal situation after Varkiza resulted in an attempt to regroup the non-Communist socialist forces in view of the political normality the country was supposed to be entering. This did not have serious repercussions in itself, for their actual political force had been marginal. What however was more significant was the fact that the Communists, left in isolation, could no longer present themselves as a broad popular coalition but were obliged to make it clear where they stood ideologically. The Zachariades leadership was later condemned for having given the movement a 'socialist-revolutionary character' which was not in tune with prevailing conditions. But it was hardly Zachariades' fault that all non-Communist elements refused to take part in the new armed struggle. Six years of continuous fighting had been enough for the majority of the people. And the National Front strategy pursued by EAM during the occupation had done little to prepare the peasants ideologically for a struggle for the installation of a Communist regime. Furthermore, the middle classes, who had mainly supported EAM during the occupation, were very much opposed to a new war. Although the economic situation could hardly be considered as normalized, the first and most urgent demand of the middle classes was economic stability and any threat of continual upheaval was dead against their interests and desires. The pre-war stratification of the urban population re-emerged at least in its outlines, and the majority of the middle classes naturally favoured a state of affairs which promised them a revival of their shattered status. The atrocities and excesses committed by the Communists during the last days of December, ably magnified by the propagandists of the Royalist governments, greatly contributed to the hesitancy of a great part of the ex-supporters of EAM. Although still enjoying the sympathies of a considerable fraction of the population who felt that the struggle was just, the KKE thus met with great resistance in launching a new war. Zisis Zographos, a member of the KKE Central Committee, later admitted that 'the decision on armed struggle ran counter to the sentiments of the masses'. Even many Party functionaries and members did not agree with it.

Just as important, however, as the attitude of the majority of EAM members was the line adopted by the Communist Party. The city organizations, the core of Communist power, were not allowed to leave the city and join the guerrillas. Strategically, guerrilla warfare was still considered subsidiary to the decisive struggle which, according to Marxist–Leninist orthodoxy, would ultimately come about in the towns. Even large military units, the composition of which was orientated to the left, were prevented from joining the Democratic Army in the mountains. The mistakes committed during the occupation were repeated on a larger scale. Apart from the fact that, until the middle of 1947, guerrilla warfare was still used by Zachariades (who was freely moving about in Athens until 1947) as a weapon to impose a political agreement, it should be taken into consideration that KKE leadership was increasingly suspicious of guerrilla leaders, who were seen as eventual threats to the monolithic structure of the party, Zachariades in 1947–9 was just as reluctant to strengthen Markos as Siantos had been to strengthen Aris during the resistance. Having launched a civil war, he refused to see the consequences of the venture. His most numerous and most trusted human reserves were to be sacrificed in camps, gaols or execution squads, without being given the opportunity to fire a single shot.

Although there is only scanty evidence for the reasons of this fatally contradictory policy, it seems that dogmatic insistence on pure Leninist theories led to disregard and open mistrust of the potentialities of the peasant movement. Markos's deputy Kikitzas told the French writer D. Eudes (in an unpublished series of interviews) that Zachariades expressly forbade the broadening of guerrilla warfare on the basis of peasant conscription and set the number of 10,000 as the maximum of guerrilla effectives (Spring, 1947). As early as June 1945, Zachariades had criticized the 'faulty composition' of the party, only 18 per cent of which were workers. He seems to have met with some success, for, in a later survey, 42 per cent were found to be members of the working class, though only 28 per cent were of 'proletarian' descent and upbringing (R. V. Burks, 'Statistical Survey of the Greek Communist', *Journal of Modern History*, XXVIII, 1955, p. 155). But the peasants who could have been mobilized on a large scale in 1946–7 were rebuffed. In 1948 even ELAS was condemned by the Communist leadership as 'petty-bourgeois deviationism', a line that could only accentuate peasant distrust. Thus, theoretical dogmatism and fear of losing Party authority combined in creating the wastage of town effectives and alienation of peasants. If this line contributed to the subsequent difficulties of the Democratic Army in building up its reserves, it also partly explains the relative ease with which the Right was to acquire a powerful grip on the rural population on the basis of an anti-Communist ideology.

Thus only a small number of the progressives were in favour of the war. This was to prove of great significance when, later on, the problem of manpower reserves came to haunt the Communist leaders. So it was only the hard-core fighters who could be trusted to obey the call to arms. The problem of supplies was also of critical importance. The few arms retained after the Varkiza Agreement could only be a provisional basis for the struggle. Complete dependence on

Yugoslavia, Bulgaria and Albania could therefore not be avoided. Although it is not known what help was promised before the war started, training camps were functioning as early as the beginning of 1946, and a significant amount of supplies was in fact given. Most important, a pledge to keep the frontier open was given, a fact which was of paramount importance for the coming guerrilla warfare.

It is true that the Greek government could hardly be considered as being in a position of strength. 'Obviously unrepresentative' according to Walter Lippman, it had neither the prestige nor the power to follow or impose a national policy. Its sole source of power was British support. Thus, when in February 1947 the British government declared that Britain was unable to continue to assist Greece and that British troops would soon have to be withdrawn, the situation looked ominous for the government. British 'protection' had constituted the foundation on which the policy of the Right had been based. The withdrawal of Britain from the Near East, so soon after her diplomatic triumph in Greece, was the first sign of the disintegration of the Empire. One hundred years of British predominance in the Eastern Mediterranean virtually ended when the growing domestic economic problems, and the shifting of the centre of the British strategic interests further to the East, obliged the Labour government to evacuate Greece. The Greek government was left alone with neither the means nor the power to preserve its position. But the power vacuum was not to last for long. Only a few days later, on 12 March 1947, the Truman Doctrine was officially announced. The United States was embarking on a new diplomacy of intervention. From now on, any left-wing threat in a country not already Communist was to be 'contained' by force, if necessary. American intervention in Greece, as stated in the Truman doctrine, was only the beginning. Guatemala, Egypt, Lebanon, Cuba, San Domingo and finally Vietnam were to follow.

The military and economic aid which poured into Greece as a result of the Truman Doctrine and of the subsequently proclaimed Marshall Plan was indeed unprecedented in amplitude. Congress approved a sum of $300 million in 1947, and much more was to come. But in addition to the quantity of US aid and its effect on the Greek economy, its first and most lasting significance was that it provided a permanent and highly efficient mechanism of intervention in Greek affairs. In contrast to the loans of the pre-war period, American aid was by and large a gift. Through bargaining over the amount and the use of the money given, the USA had a stronger hold over Greek governments than Britain had ever managed to get. An implied threat to stop, reduce or even postpone the aid was enough to make Greek ministers fall flat on their faces. This goes far to explain the ease with which the USA could impose governments, policies and personalities even after the civil war was over. This was a change from the past. British influence had been based on an elaborate and carefully developed system of 'agents' – either paid or, more often, unpaid – who possessed or acquired key positions in the decision-making processes of Greece. Under normal circumstances, British intervention was never blatant or explicit, since it was channelled through diplomatic and 'covered' activities. American influence, on the contrary, soon became a recognized institution.

Thus the octagenarian Liberal Sophoulis was imposed as Prime Minister once again, heading a government based on a Royalist parliamentary majority. American intervention in the installation of the Sophoulis government was exceptionally blunt. The Prime Minister and leader of the parliamentary majority, Tsaldaris, was summoned and told that all aid would be withdrawn if he did not resign and make room for the already concocted Sophoulis coalition within twenty-four hours. Tsaldaris gave in and the new government, repeatedly reshuffled, lasted until the end of the civil war.

When, in January 1948, a political crisis again seemed imminent, US Ambassador Griswold did not hesitate to threaten the political world that 'they should renounce all attempts to form a new coalition, because the existing coalition is the last possible parliamentary solution.' A new crisis would lead 'to an *extra-parliamentary solution*, which would eventually be considered dictatorial'. In such a case the USA might reconsider its policy on aid.

This period marks the definite re-establishment of the pre-war political patterns. Liberals and Populists re-emerged as the major political groupings of the Centre and Right respectively, and were split into many small personal parties. The main change brought about by the civil war was that they both accepted the monarchy unreservedly. Both consistently yielded to American pressure and joined in coalition governments. Under the impact of the civil war and American aid, differences of ideology and policy between them quickly evaporated. Each hailed US aid and intervention, but for different reasons. The Right saw its control over the Army and the civil service strengthened as never before, while the Centre hoped that the American desire for attractive-looking compromises would give it the lion's share of political office, since a vacuum was left by the civil war and the discrediting of both the Communists and the moderate Left.

This void was the more complete because the 1946 election was boycotted by the Communists, the Socialists and the more progressive faction of the Liberals. When the civil war began, the parties which did have seats in the Assembly naturally tried to monopolize the scene. The bitterness of the civil war was so great that they succeeded. By 1948 there was no other alternative. It was either pro or anti-Communism. Most of the non-Communist progressive forces that had stayed out of Parliament during that critical period found themselves completely powerless to influence events. Their audience dwindled and the first chance Greece had to form a socialist party vanished. In the days of dark oppression that were to come, it was easy for the right-wing propagandists to identify the Communists with the non-Communist left. After all, EAM had been a joint venture. The moderate progressive forces also found themselves completely alienated from the Communists, who could never forgive the fact that they had been abandoned at a crucial moment. Although a great number of non-Communists had suffered and were to suffer in the concentration camps as the result of the white terror, they were still snubbed as traitors. Isolated as it was between two factions of the nation in bitter struggle with one another, the Greek socialist movement was doomed. It would take almost twenty years for a similar movement to revive, under completely different circumstances.

The first period of the civil war, from February 1946, which is regarded as the official opening date, till the spring of 1947, was confined to an extended build-up. Communist activities were limited to scattered assaults on small and isolated villages and military units throughout the country. Still weak in numbers, the Communist guerrilla bands could not achieve anything more than the spreading of a climate of insecurity and terror in the countryside. When in August 1946 General Markos Vafiades was sent into the mountains to organize and coordinate guerrilla activities, he was confronted with serious difficulties. He was very short of men, supplies and ammunition. Although the Greek regular Army was not yet in action, the National Guard of about 50,000 men, with the help of the still numerous right-wing bands, was sufficient to keep the Communists restricted to marginal activity. Markos, an able strategist, opted for the hit-and-run tactics which he was to follow up to the end, while doing all he could to strengthen his forces, which amounted at the outset to no more than 4,000 men. Gradually, though with much less enthusiasm than during the German occupation, many former ELAS fighters joined him. But the numbers were still inadequate and Markos was driven by necessity to the recruitment of villagers. This process, which was to constitute the basis of Markos's army, was voluntary to begin with but gradually took on a more and more forcible character. Men and women fought side by side, the proportion of the latter growing and finally reaching 25 per cent. This method of recruitment, though it served its purpose by enabling Markos to develop an army 20,000 strong, had considerable defects. Most of the recruits were untrained village people and needed a long period of training. Although Yugoslavia contributed training camps, this increased the logistic dependence on Tito and kept the Communist Army widely dispersed. The bravery and tenacity which some of these recruits were to show later on could not counterbalance their military inexperience. When in 1949 guerrilla tactics were abandoned in favour of conventional warfare, the scarcity of professionally trained personnel would be bitterly felt.

The regular Army, on the other hand, although reorganized by the British Military Mission, was still in an unsatisfactory state. Although by 1946 it numbered about 100,000 men, it was badly equipped, insufficiently mobile and suffered from an over-centralized and incompetent command. Up to the middle of 1947 it did not take part in military operations and indulged in 'static defence' of the cities and communications centres which it controlled.

Thus, when, in the spring of 1947, Markos intensified guerrilla warfare, the Army was hardly in a position to counter-attack. Raids became more frequent and the majority of the countryside seemed to be under Communist control. Partly encouraged by his successes and partly under the pressure of the Yugoslavs and Bulgarians, Markos launched a series of attacks on a larger scale against the towns of Florina, Konitsa, Kastoria, Grevena and Alexandroupolis. The object was to capture a town in which a rival Greek government could be established and recognized by the Communist nations. All these attacks failed and made a return to guerrilla tactics necessary, but they convinced the Americans that their intervention had to be more massive. Another influence was the intensification of the cold war, which became 'official' for the first time with battles in the UN over the Greek issue between the US and the USSR, and in particular with the creation of the Cominform in October 1947. By the end of that year suplies were pouring in, and the US Military Mission (JUSMAPG) assumed the strategic leadership over the head of the Joint US–Greek Staff, hitherto responsible for planning and supplying military operations. The effects on the regular army were far-reaching. It was enlarged to 200,000 men; special anti-guerrilla mountain divisions were trained; the Army was supplied with modern weapons, artillery, napalm bombs, tanks and aircraft. A modern network of communications was created. Airfields, roads, bridges and ports which had been out of use since the German occupation were speedily repaired.

Nevertheless, throughout 1948 and notwithstanding the launching of large-scale offensives, the Army did not manage to break the guerrillas. Although casualties were very high, Markos successfully kept up his tactics, hitting hard when not expected, retreating and even crossing the international northern border when unduly pressed. In the military sense, 1948 proved to be a stalemate, neither side managing to win considerable advantages over the other.

However, the balance of forces had radically changed. For the hope of the Communists that a general insurrection within the towns would in due course enable their military forces to break the undermined governmental forces was disappointed. The hardening of police action against Communists, the outlawing of the Communist Party and the arrest of thousands of members had resulted in the shattering of the Communist network within the cities. Thousands of persons were arrested, tried and executed for minor or non-existent offences. (The exact number of executions has not been disclosed.) Selective conscription, which had been the basis of the Greek Army and which left the bulk of leftists free in the cities, had been abandoned, and by now all young Communist sympathizers were called up – only to be separated from the rest of the Army and interned in the notorious concentration camps of Makronissos and Youra. Communist strength in the cities was completely broken. This knocked the props from under the Communist strategy of taking control after weakening the government by intensified guerrilla warfare. Time was now working against them. The Army was gradually becoming a formidable machine, constantly growing in numbers, weapons and supplies. Recruitment for the guerrillas was steadily getting more difficult, as the government started to move peasants in great numbers from areas subject to Communist raids into quieter regions.

But the decisive event that foreshadowed the Communist defeat occurred on 28 June 1948. Following the deepening rift between Stalin and Tito, Yugoslavia was expelled from the Cominform. This posed a frightful dilemma for the Greek Communists. Yugoslavia was their main supply centre, and it was over the Yugoslav border that Markos's troops usually retreated when in peril. But Russia, though she had offered little actual help, was the mother country to which the hard-core Communists – Zachariades especially – felt unquestioning obedience. For the time being – indeed for a whole year – they did not have to take a stand. Tito kept up his assistance and the Soviet Union did not require Zachariades to disavow him. But the situation had become extremely precarious.

It was thus political more than purely military difficulties that started to demoralize the Democratic Army. As the countryside was being emptied, the Communists intensified their terrorist raids and resumed the practice of taking hostages, even though these same practices had been officially condemned by the Communist leadership when they had occurred in December 1944. These excesses and especially the removal of children between the ages of three and fourteen (most of them related to guerrilla fighters recruited either willingly or forcedly) and expatriating them to Yugoslavia and Bulgaria did much to discredit the Communist cause. They evoked the darkest days of Ottoman rule in the Balkans, when the Turks periodically rounded up Christian children and made them into Janissaries. Every Greek schoolboy is taught to shrink at the idea of 'children-snatching', the symbol of foreign and tyrannical oppression, and the propaganda instruments of the government made the most of the historical parallel.

Probably the greatest political mistake of the Communists, however, was to revive the problem of the Macedonian minorities. Although the population of Greek Macedonia had been predominantly Greek since the massive influx of immigrants from Asia Minor, due to Venizelos, the Communist Party had repeatedly raised the question of a separate Macedonian nation. Already in December 1947 the 'Provisional Democratic Government' had underlined the significance of a national minority by creating a special committee to treat the problem directly under Prime Minister Markos. In January

1949, at the 5th Plenum of the Greek Communist Party, Zachariades posed the question once more, obviously under pressure of the Bulgarians, whose support was by now of critical importance. 'The Macedonian population', runs the official decision, 'which has fought valiantly on the side of the Greek Communists, should be protected in its interests against the Greek chauvinists who oppress their national rights.' Probably more than anything else, the resurgence of the Macedonian question, which had been haunting Greek foreign policy for fifty years, contributed to the effectiveness of the ideological arsenal of the Right. The all too fresh memories of Bulgarian atrocities during the Axis occupation fed the reviving slavophobia with horrible connotations, especially among the peasants along the northern frontier, where the main battles were being fought. Far from feeling like 'fish in the water' the guerrillas were by now encountering open mistrust and enmity from the peasant population they depended on.

The turn of the year marked another significant modification in military operations. Pressed by time, now that Tito's support was no longer certain, Zachariades decided against Markos's express protests to change Communist tactics from guerrilla to conventional warfare. The small, independent and self-sufficient units that had so successfully resisted the Army were grouped into brigades of considerable strength. The all-or-nothing fight that could only result from this change in tactics speaks for the disarray of the Communist leadership. Markos was subsequently dismissed 'for reasons of health' and Zachariades assumed the military and political leadership personally.

In the meantime, the reorganization of the Army was further pursued. Under American pressure, the officer corps was completely reshuffled, younger and more energetic officers were entrusted with senior posts and on 25 February 1949 General Papagos, military commander in the Albanian war of 1940, was appointed Commander-in-Chief of armed forces and was given practically dictatorial authority. The cumulative effect of these changes proved decisive. In the spring of 1949 large clearing operations were undertaken by a rejuvenated and well-equipped Army. By the middle of March the Peloponnese was completely cleared of guerrillas and in April large Army forces moved into Roumeli (Central Greece), which after bitter fighting they also managed to clear. The Communists were by now restricted to the mountains of northern Greece, along the border. A new attack against Florina failed, while the guerrilla army could no longer replace its casualties with new recruits. The impact of conventional warfare was disastrous on the Communists. The inferiority in men and equipment which was of lesser importance during the guerrilla phase was now deadly. The problem of maintenance of a permanent network of supplies proved insurmountable. New offers for negotiations were turned down by the government and a heavy governmental attack on the Kaimakchalan mountains on the Yugoslav border in the beginning of July virtually divided the Communist forces in two. Thus, when on 10 July Tito announced the closing of the Yugoslav border, he was administering the *coup de grâce*. Apart from minor forces on the Bulgarian border, which were broken up in the beginning of August, the Communist forces were restricted to the triangular area adjacent to the point where Greece, Yugoslavia and Albania meet. A general offensive against the Grammos and Vitsi mountain ranges that dominate the region was launched in August. The battles were long and bitter, but by the end of the month the remnants of the Democratic Army were pushed behind the Albanian border. To all intents and purposes the civil war had ended. Two months later, on 16 October 1949, the Communist Party announced its decision to cease fire.

CHAPTER 8

The Aftermath of the Civil War and the Liberal Failure (1949–52)

ACCORDING to official figures, the civil war cost 40,000 lives. Unofficial estimates range up to 158,000. Hundreds of thousands of people were made homeless, and the material damage reduced the country to a state not much better than in 1944. Another 80,000 or 100,000 people crossed the border as refugees and were gradually absorbed in the various Communist countries, the largest colony being at Tashkent in Central Asia. Yet in the final analysis the decisive legacy of the civil war was not the enormous human and material disaster, but the unprecedented political, ideological and cultural cleavage between what was labelled 'the national attitude' on the one hand, and the remnants of the progressive forces on the other.

If the inevitable aftermath of any civil war is repression of the defeated by the victors, in Greece the repression went beyond the scope of politics. Not only were the victims expelled, persecuted and exterminated, but also, as in Spain, the post-war regime imposed its culture as well as its material power. However, unlike Franco's Spain, Greece remained – in the formal sense, at least – a democracy. The effects of this phenomenon are hard to measure or to define. The new medieval ethos that blanketed the country was not imposed solely by force, but was brought about through the cleavage that operated on the political level.

If any culture is in its essence a class culture, in the sense that it represents the attitudes and outlook of the dominant group in society, the mechanisms for minimizing or emasculating dissent usually work through control of information – or, more subtly, by capturing dissident ideas and assimilating them within the system itself. But the specific feature of the Greek cultural system was that criticism and dissent were forcibly reduced to total silence by the class in power; all fundamental political and social alternatives were banished. The gradual evaporation of the vestiges of the 'Great Idea' after 1922 had cut the ground from under the feet of the developing bourgeoisie; and, during the inter-war period, the ruling class had been prevented from establishing a stable ideological frame of reference by a combination of innate incapacity and international events. The very little that had been added by the progressive forces had been shattered by the long years of dictatorship, occupation and resistance. Thus, with the obliteration of the Communist Party in 1949, following upon the deep disarray into which the whole progressive movement had fallen in 1945, the end of the civil war left Greece with nothing to balance the political domination of the victorious Right – which had nothing to offer save political and military power. If anti-Communism as a political outlook was the common denominator of the 'free world', in Greece it permeated every aspect of social and cultural life.

Politically, the cleavage was total. The Left had been beaten and blown to bits. Thousands of the people who had constituted the nation's progressive élite had been killed, imprisoned or exiled. The hecatomb can only be compared with the sombre fate of the Spanish intelligentsia. It is true that the Left was eventually allowed political representation. But the creation of EDA (United Democratic Left) in 1951 only served to neutralize the dissident movement more effectively. An impenetrable ideological and political ghetto was developed, and the Left was still completely cut off from the life of the rest of the country. In organizing political affairs, left-wing votes did not count. Any non-Communist group that tried to collaborate with the Left was at once discredited and disowned. The slim body of non-Communist but socialist thought was quickly swallowed up by this process. Those who stood firmly by their beliefs were reduced to political non-existence, while the less high-principled were absorbed by the Liberals. Dissidents were silenced one after the other, and for many years – until the early 1960s – there was no grouping, newspaper or periodical advocating a non-Communist alternative to reaction in the political, social or cultural sphere.

Meanwhile, the isolation of the Communists only intensified their hardening of the ideological arteries. Deprived of their red banner (the Communist Party had been banned since 1947) they were obliged to pursue an officially reformist political line. But their need to maintain ideological rigidity, combined with the constant pressure that perpetuated their isolation, made for the development of an even more stringent orthodoxy in their cultural attitude. EDA recruited a number of non-Communist politicians who refused to conform to the *status quo*, but it was hardly an attraction for the gradually emerging new intelligentsia, to whom rigid Zhdanovism (the Stalinist policy of imposing the party line on all scientific, intellectual or artistic activities) offered at least a dubious appeal. However, with the exception of EDA – which, despite its isolation, could at least function as a coherent ideological group – there was no possible platform for the expression of new ideas. This total cleavage accounts to a significant extent for the inward-looking and non-political character of non-Communist culture in the years that followed the civil war, despite the acuteness of the social problems that had emerged. It is no coincidence that, while Greeks forged ahead in the visual arts, in music and in poetry, there were no major achievements in the social sciences, literary criticism or prose writing. Not merely political opposition, but any kind of dissident progressive outlook, was at once identified by the dominant bourgeoisie with Communist-inspired subversiveness. Though secular in its essence, modern Greek culture retained considerable religious overtones, and no major anticlerical trend managed to escape the prevailing conformity. Though mainly oriented toward the West, Greece was unwilling to take a share in the flourishing of critical and demystifying thought that followed the Second World War in Western Europe. Major novelists, who had expressed their national and cultural searchings in the Greece that had emerged from the 1922 catastrophe, now rewrote their novels in expurgated versions. A number of the most talented thinkers, such as Kazantzakis, turned – brilliantly, be it said – to problems of metaphysical ethography and turned their backs on the concrete, modern Greek reality.

These trends were already inherent in the castrated efforts of the Greek ruling class to find an image of itself in the 1930s. But the civil war led to the culmination of the rampant process that undermined the cultural life of the country. The timid modernizing changes that had been imposed on the antiquated educational system by Venizelos in the early thirties were reversed. Greek and international history is now taught only up to the end of the First World War, and the resistance against the Germans is either systematically ignored or continually discredited. Within the context of a secular education, religion and scripture are compulsory subjects for all schoolchildren for twelve years. Ancient Greek grammar is taught on every single day throughout the secondary schools, but the content of ancient texts is never analysed or even discussed. In higher education, the situation is even sadder. While technical schools lack modern facilities and research laboratories because funds are inadequate, the position in the Humanities is downright obscurantist. Some years ago – and to this day, most probably – the only mention of Freud in the Philosophical Faculty of Athens University was in a footnote in which he is referred to as an authority on dreams. Marx is of course anathema, and sociology is an unknown scientific discipline. The history of philosophy ends with Kant. Even Darwin was recently attacked by a supposedly serious Athens newspaper as a carrier of dangerous subversive ideas.

Thus, the search for a national identity, which had been the major preoccupation of the Greek ruling class throughout the nineteenth century, had finally and sadly failed. It was the realization of this failure that had been the main stimulant for the search for new directions during the thirties, and this in turn had found its political counterpart in the resistance against the Germans. During and after the civil war, when this vast movement of intellectual awakening had to be checked, anti-Communism presented itself as a general-purpose ideology to justify the regression into the dried-up womb of

Greco–Christian traditions.' Thus the civil war served to perpetuate the bondage of a system that was already naturally exhausted, frustrated and incapable of any dynamic development. It provided the unifying link and the *raison d'être* for a cultural system that had irretrievably lost all points of reference. And in the end it managed to create yet another 'lost generation'.

The purity of the language was protected in the name of anti-Communism, and so was Christianity as an obligatory social framework. Any fundamental criticism of social, moral or legal institutions was banned or kept for better days. The new Constitution, promulgated in 1952, preached liberty of conscience and declared the separation of State and Church – but opened with the words: 'The dominant religion in Greece is the Eastern Orthodox Church of Christ.' Religious marriage is the only form that one can legally contract in Greece. Significantly enough, it was not the Church – whose power is minimal – that imposed this new theocracy; it was the conscious choice of the groups in power. Emerging after the war shattered, self-centred and fearful, the only cultural reference points the ruling class could propose were those of the past, which was resurrected by all means possible. The necessary counterpoint of this renewed glorification of 'tradition' was the identification of novelty and intellectual integrity with subversion. Typically, pure and eternal values were invoked only to draw the line between anti-Communism and the 'evil' of dissent when a threat to cultural orthodoxy was present. The kiosks of Athens swarmed with Parisian pornographic magazines, yet Sartre's *Le Mur* was banned as obscene.

Thus, curiously enough, the deep political and ideological gulf between 'national' and Communist Greece coincided with a striking conformity of views, whenever the issues were not immediately political. Zhdanovism is not so far away from a commonplace obscurantist cultural dictatorship. While they fought to the death, both sides were probably unaware of how essentially similar would be the consequences of their competing forms of conservatism. The civil war had polarized Greek culture to the point where monopoly by the victors was actually helped by the intolerance of their victims. It would take the emergence of a new generation to break the deadlock.

But, in the last analysis, the cultural and ideological repercussions outlined above were only a function of the political development that followed the end of the civil war. Certainly, there was no escaping the polarization of political forces into two self-negating and incompatible groups. However, it was a matter of deliberate choice whether political power would seek to heal or to maintain the new national schism. Although there can be no doubt that by 1949 the overwhelming majority of Greeks were more rather than less anti-Communist, and were fully convinced of the need to guard the country from any renewed attempt at rebellion, it is also undeniable that most Greeks were deeply conscious of the dangers that threatened if the 'schism' became permanent.

To appreciate the significance of the shifting names of people and parties during an extremely unstable yet homogeneous period of history, it must be recalled that the abstention of the Left in the 1946 election had produced an unrepresentative right-wing Parliament, but that British and American pressure during the civil war imposed Centre-dominated governments under Liberal Prime Ministers. Oddly enough, in these exceptional conditions, the government was more representative of the popular will than the Parliament. This paradox became more evident after the end of the civil war. And it was not confined to the top of the political structure. The people voiced the need for stability, reconstruction and above all what soon became the slogan of the Liberals: Lethe (forgetfulness) and Amnesty. But in the Army and the administration, not to speak of the private sector and the grey area where relief was controlled, the key posts were almost exclusively occupied by the right-wing extremists who had obtained them during the Royalist revival of 1944–7. It is the constant struggle for control of policy-making at all levels, and the repercussions of changes in the aims of US policy, that explain how – despite the overwhelming popular desire for a moderate national policy, which made the Liberals the natural governing party – they presided instead over a gradually more disappointed and unstable political scene, and unwittingly laid the basis for a long period of right-wing rule.

However, lest misplaced emphasis should be given to the elements of instability and malaise, attention must be drawn to the unique fact of a demand for moderation after the end of a full-blown civil war. The only explanation of this incredible phenomenon was that victory over Communist revolution owed nothing to the patriotism of the governing classes. If Communist excesses gave rise to the profound desire for political stability and personal security, the injustice and corruption met with at the hands of the old ruling class – not to mention its collaboration with the Germans or its support for the pre-war Metaxas dictatorship – were neither forgotten nor forgiven.

The social issue that was consistently behind the resistance to the Germans was of such long standing and so deeply ingrained in popular consciousness that it survived the holocaust of 1944, was inflamed by the white terror, and again survived the civil war, to re-emerge as a demand in the 1949 election and indeed ever since. Thus, to sum up the entire paradox: the Greek civil war stemmed from right-wing reaction. It was fought and won by progressives. They then tried in vain to blunt its effects as well as to remove what had been its acutest causes. Instead, they paved the way for the return of the same right-wing reaction, which methodically rebuilt the structure of social inequality that had caused the original explosion.

But this is looking ahead. In 1949, the US State Department was fully conscious of the trends that had emerged from the civil war. It was also in a position of strength. Economically, the country had been ruined; American aid had enabled the government to function and ultimately to win the war. But the economic problems were actually aggravated and complicated when peace came. Dollars would have to flow in continuously if a minimum of normality was to be restored.

The Americans favoured a government as representative of the people as possible. No section of the political world questioned the assumption that Greece had to depend on US protection, so the broadening of the government to include more conciliatory tendencies was encouraged – and, later on, openly dictated – by the US.

Threats of curtailment or cutting off of economic aid constituted, throughout this period, the method by which the Americans imposed their views. Thus, when the Liberal leader Sophoulis died in June 1949 and the coalition between Populists and Liberals showed signs of breaking up, Ambassador Grady announced that in the opinion of the US it was time to hold another election. The end of the war and the imposed reconciliation between the two main political groups should now be sanctioned by popular vote. And, the Americans thought, it was time to elect a Parliament more representative than that of 1946.

The election was held on 5 March 1950. The Liberals, advocating moderation, won a clear majority. But their division into numerous hostile factions, of which the most important were led by Plastiras, Sophocles Venizelos and George Papandreou, made it extremely difficult to achieve an effective coalition. The issue of a general amnesty separated the right-wingers under Venizelos from the left-wingers under Plastiras. In fact, personal incompatibilities played a greater role than policy differences. Venizelos, refusing to work with Plastiras, formed a government in collaboration with the Right. But American intervention brought about his downfall and imposed a broader coalition under Plastiras.

The Plastiras government lasted for almost eight months. It was the country's first chance to implement a policy of reconciliation and heal the wounds of war. But Plastiras was scarcely the man to cope with the very difficult conditions. Pure and honest, but of limited intelligence, he felt ill at ease in the climate of backstage manoeuvres and compromises in which he was entangled. Not being able to impose his views, he only managed to expose his prestige. The problems of economic reconstruction rapidly swallowed up the more general issues of home policy. Plastiras was undermined and soon overshadowed by masters of the parliamentary game – Venizelos, Papandreou and the other professional politicians whom he was obliged to include in his cabinet. The disastrous economic situation showed no sign of recovery. The dilemma of yielding to demands for higher wages and containing the galloping inflationary trends was beyond the abilities of the ageing general. In the end he resigned – a confession of failure.

There followed a chaotic period of perpetual realignment of coalitions and cabinets. For almost another year Venizelos managed to retain the Premiership, supported first by right-wingers and later by left-wingers. Endemic problems and governmental instability combined to make the difficulties of reconstruction even greater. Throughout 1950 and 1951 the situation could hardly have been worse. Unemployment stood at about 20 per cent of the registered workers, reconstruction was taking its time, owing to the government's inability to control the magnates who had taken over the channels of aid distribution since 1945, and, especially after Plastiras departed, repression set in once more. No coherent reform programme was presented in the political chaos that marked the Liberals' inability to offer a stable and firmly oriented leadership.

In the meantime, however, serious international developments had taken place. The Korean war had broken out in May 1950 and the consequent tendency to harden anti-Communist positions on the home fronts, which also found its counterpart in the rise of McCarthyism in the United States, led to a shift in the policy of the US towards Greece. Much more than for a broadly based democratic government, strategic and political considerations called for rigorous internal stability and anti-Communist vigilance. Plastiras had not only proved incapable of imposing a disciplined administration, he was also honestly and above all concerned with ending the cleavage that had resulted from the civil war. In view, however, of the international situation, such luxurious preoccupations were not only superfluous; by degrees, they became undesirable.

This new US outlook was marked by the replacement of the affable Grady by John Peurifoy as Ambassador. Peurifoy, who had already made himself a name as a tough operator, came to Greece with a specific mission: to bring about a powerful, stable and uncompromisingly anti-Communist government. His first step was to bring about a reorganization of the Right, which under the feeble leadership of Tsaldaris had allowed the powerful position of the Royalist party to evaporate. Field-Marshal Papagos, the military leader of the Royalist faction during the thirties, Metaxas's main supporter, hero of the Albanian campaign and Commander-in-Chief of the national Greek Army during the last victorious phase of the civil war, was suddenly persuaded to enter the political arena. The venture was a sensational success. The new party was called 'The Greek Rally', as Papagos attempted to draw a parallel between Greek and French problems and pose as the nation's saviour in the manner of de Gaulle. He did not refrain from making the well-known claim that his movement was above and beyond parties. Nevertheless, it worked. Papagos was quickly surrounded by the majority of the political personnel of the Right, as well as by a considerable number of Liberal politicians who sensed the rising star. Public opinion was on the whole positively impressed and the press was enthusiastic. The first phase of Peurifoy's plan had thus been easily fulfilled. For his next step he only had to bid for time.

With one governmental crisis following another, it was inevitable that new elections should take place soon. They were held in September 1951 and Papagos naturally emerged as the new favourite, with 36.5 per cent of the votes. The scattered remnants of the former Right, amongst them the Populists, virtually disappeared. The need for governmental stability was universally felt and the constantly reshuffled Liberal governments were greatly discredited. Yet if Papagos had shown his strength, over 60 per cent of the population still preferred to go on trying to find a more moderate solution. For despite his well-publicized inadequacies, General Plastiras's pacificatory voice was not ignored. With 23.5 per cent of the votes, he supplanted Venizelos as leader of the most powerful Centre formation, even though he suffered virulent attacks from the Left, which had by then re-emerged under the name of EDA, obtaining 9 per cent of the vote. By identifying Plastiras with

Papagos in their electoral slogans, EDA, while hardly strengthening their own position, contributed to the effectiveness of the political ghetto their adversaries were diligently building up. Plastiras, and after him a number of leaders who aspired to create the prerequisites of a coherent democratic movement, were rejected by the Left they hoped to embrace. The forces that were willing to fight for the abolition of the already ominous cleavage were thwarted both from the Right and from the Left.

It was only because of Papagos's adamant refusal to accept any coalition that Venizelos, who did not hide his preference for cooperation with him, was obliged willy-nilly to serve under a government led by Plastiras. This last Liberal government did not last more than a year. It was to be the swan song of the Liberals. They would not return to power for another twelve years.

The last Liberal administration was as unsuccessful as the previous ones. Constantly sabotaged by the reluctant Vice-Premier Venizelos on the question of amnesty and reconciliation, Plastiras was once more forced to do without the social cornerstone of his mandate. Moreover, in March 1952 he fell seriously ill. Though still nominally Prime Minister he was in practice replaced by Venizelos.

The undisguised distrust shown by the US towards the new government further precipitated its centrifugal tendencies. As early as January, a sharp reduction of US aid had multiplied economic difficulties and the task of reconstruction appeared to be deadlocked. Venizelos's decision to turn for support to the King did not open new possibilities. Playing on the fact of Anglo–American antagonism, which was once more in the air, he placed his bet on the wrong horse by turning to London for support. Even King Paul's favour, which was thus secured, and the King's personal grudge against Papagos, whose authority threatened to endanger the Palace's interventionary powers, could not tip the balance in Venizelos's favour. For the USA, whose aid was a day-to-day necessity, had decided to back the Greek Rally. Venizelos's manoeuvres were entirely in vain. His attempt to appease American disfavour by passing anti-Communist laws only served to lay the foundations for the eventual right-wing political monopoly. Venizelos's laws and police measures intensified the repression, concentration camps were set up on a permanent basis, and a large number of Communists were executed. All this served to deepen the malaise of the Liberal electorate and strongly alienate its progressive wing. Split into irreconcilable factions, lacking – after Plastiras had in effect retired – a leader who enjoyed prestige and general acceptance, and incapable of facing the economic problems of reconstruction, the Centre was losing its grip in every respect.

Peurifoy's chance to hasten the return of the Right to power came in March 1952, when a serious controversy arose over the electoral system to be used in the forthcoming election. (Any system, to be adopted, had to have majority support in Parliament.) Most of the shrewd Centre politicians favoured proportional representation, which would work out not too badly for the small parties to which they belonged. However, it became clear that Plastiras, either through senile miscalculation or in a gesture of throwing down the gauntlet, was inclined towards the majority system. Peurifoy thereupon acted promptly. He publicly declared: 'The US Government believes that the re-establishment of the simple proportional system, with its unavoidable consequences of the continuation of governmental instability, would have destructive results upon the effective utilization of US aid to Greece. The US Embassy feels itself obliged (he went on, attempting to sweeten the pill) to make its support publicly known for the patriotic position of Prime Minister Plastiras on this subject.' Lest this should not prove to be enough, he also threatened behind the scenes to suspend US aid if the proportional system were accepted. The government gave in and the majority system was voted. Peurifoy and Papagos only had to wait for an opportunity to press for new elections.

The chance came in the autumn. Pressed by the need for economies and suffering from a continued embargo of American aid, Plastiras opted for reducing military expenditure by some 35 million dollars. Reactions were immediate. Both

Papagos and the US accused Plastiras of endangering the defensive potential of the country. Two centrist deputies deserted the government and joined Papagos, thus creating a problem of parliamentary balance as the government's majority was extremely slim. The balance was momentarily restored when two deputies from EDA joined Plastiras's party. But Peurifoy had not played his last trump. In an unprecedentedly blatant statement to the Greek press, he expressed the opinion that

> owing to the rapid political developments and the fact that the EPEK [Plastiras's party] has replaced two of its members with ex-EDA leftists, it is my recommendation that the best thing for Greece would be to have new elections under the majority system as soon as possible.

For all the crudeness of Peurifoy's language, the ageing Prime Minister accepted the inevitable. On 16 November 1952 general elections took place for the third time in two years. Papagos won 49.2 per cent of the votes, but, through the operation of the majority system, he obtained 82.3 per cent of the seats in Parliament. Peurifoy's mission was thus completed. He had been the architect of the process of undermining the Liberals, and had organized the return of the Right to power.[1] US economic blackmail and open intervention had complemented the failings of the Liberal governments. Greece was entering a phase of conservative stability – alas, a deadly one.

1. One year later he was selected to organize the *coup d'état* that brought down the leftist government in Guatemala and installed the dictatorship of Castillio Armas. There again he was successful. Eventually he was to meet his Waterloo in the form of a 'mysterious' car crash in South-East Asia.

CHAPTER 9

Conservative 'Stability' – Social and Economic (1952–63)

In the twelve years between 1952 and 1963 the face of the country changed significantly. An unprecedented growth of the urban population made it, for the first time in Greek history, slightly larger than the rural population. In the 1951 census the urban population was 37.7 per cent of the total. By the 1961 census the urban population had reached 43 per cent, rural population had fallen to 44 per cent and the semi-urban had remained constant at 13 per cent. This major shift was mainly due to the rapid growth of the Athens agglomeration, which in fact absorbed 62.7 per cent of the total population increase between the two censuses and by 1961 was greater than the total urban population of the rest of the country. With the exception of Salonica (in the north) no other urban centre of any importance emerged, and the preponderance of Athens became overwhelming in all sectors of economic and social life. By 1961 the region of the capital provided over one half of industrial employment, received 80 per cent of imports, paid 75 per cent of direct and 65 per cent of indirect taxation, had an income over 40 per cent higher than the national average, absorbed over a half of total newspaper circulation, accounted for a majority of hospital beds and 85 per cent of specialist doctors and housed the bulk of the fairly excessive civil service personnel.

However, like all the swollen capitals of underdeveloped countries, Athens is not an industrial town despite its size and growth. Less than a third of its registered 'active' population is employed in industry. Of these, almost a half are employed in units of less than ten persons, usually family enterprises of a primitive character. Over two-thirds of those registered as 'active', and perhaps up to a half more who are not registered at all, form the typical overgrown service sector encountered in all developing countries. The emergence of a class of semi-independent small traders, intermediaries and casual workers, who make up the vast majority of the urban population, is probably the most important change in Greek society since the influx of the immigrants from Asia Minor. With only a third of the active population of Athens classed as wage-earners, and a smaller number in the other towns, it becomes evident that these rapidly growing groups of town-dwellers found themselves fluctuating between a petty-bourgeois and a *lumpenproletariat* way of life.

Despite the vast internal population movements, there was no clear-cut social class which was finding new means of livelihood and changing its way of life from primitive to modern. Between 1956 and 1961, 220,000 persons came to Athens from the provinces, and of these 66 per cent came from strictly rural areas. More significant, however, is the lack of any great differences in the occupations of the newcomers and of the original city population. In Athens, 30.9 per cent of immigrants and 30.8 per cent of the original population were employed in industry (in the other large towns, 31.2 per cent and 28.5 per cent respectively). In Athens, again, the original population was more strongly represented in commerce (17.9 to 10.5 per cent) but less strongly in 'other' services (25.3 to 31 per cent) and, as one would expect, in building (7.9 to 11.7 per cent). Most significantly, the rate of unemployment between the two groups is remarkably similar. Thus, in marked contrast to the inter-war problem of assimilating the Asia Minor immigrants, the new internal migrants were more or less automatically merged with the urban working class and with the remnants of the pre-war middle class, which had been largely destroyed during the occupation and the civil war.

Hence the movement from the countryside to the towns, and the wave of emigration which replaced it later in the decade, were overshadowed by larger changes: changes in employment, in consumption patterns, and in government policies to stabilize and then to develop the economy.

Economic 'reconstruction' was initially the term used for what later became 'development'. Until Papagos came to power, and especially during the civil war years, the problem was how to stop a galloping inflation. At a later stage, it was how to prevent the balance of payments from bursting. Throughout, it was necessary to give relief to homeless and hungry people, as well as to get industry and the infrastructure working again. When plans were drawn up, it was just as important to find the skilled manpower to put them into effect. The administrative system which the Liberals had built up in their heyday had been eroded by Metaxas and almost destroyed by the occupation. Up to the end of the civil war, administration was virtually taken over by the foreign economic missions. In this atmosphere, it is not surprising that most major projects of reconstruction or development, which were to be financed by war reparations or foreign aid and loans, came to little. For the foreign economic missions not only did not encourage industrialization but even fought against it. When, in 1949, a steel mill was given to Greece by the Germans as part of the war reparations, Paul Porter, chief of the US economic mission, imposed his veto. The machinery never left Hamburg and was eventually sold on behalf of the Greek government as scrap. According to the former representative of Greece to the OECD Professor Nicolaides,

> industrialization met with unrestrained reaction mainly because of its effects on the foreign trade of the interested countries, but also largely because of the economic self-sufficiency of Greece, which would have resulted from it, in a few years' time. Thus it was commercial, economic and *political* interests that imposed on the countries that took part [in the economic missions] an unqualified hostility towards all plans for Greek industrialization. (*Nea Oikonomia*, June 1956; italics in original)

The attitude of foreign economic missions ran parallel to the anarchic use of the few available funds that characterized the immediate post-war period. It is largely here that the growth of parasitic activity must be traced.

Housing and commerce yielded higher returns with less insecurity than industry. If the economic system proper did not provide productive employment, people had to fend for themselves on an *ad hoc* basis. The inventive Mediterranean mind was quick to 'discover' new products, new technologies, new services and new professions. Innumerable persons managed to make a more or less parasitic living on the fringes of the productive system. Small commerce, handicrafts, personal services of all kinds and various intermediary activities (often connected with a para-administrative complex through which the citizen could approach a lethargic and incompetent civil service) involved hundreds of thousands of people. With the passage of time this mode of existence became more or less stabilized. Out of the gradual stratification of those who 'made it', a new and extended parasitic middle class evolved. Though salaried employees accounted for a gradually increasing part of these new strata, persistent high unemployment (up to 20 per cent of urban active population) and the consequent excessive occupational mobility impeded the formation of a new solid middle class. It was only towards the end of the fifties and throughout the sixties that rapid economic growth led to the emergence of a distinguishable layer of technicians, executives, members of the liberal professions, administrators and intellectuals. These new 'professional' groupings were quite distinct from the established middle class and particularly from the 'oligarchy'. Their emergence as a social force was to coincide with the popular movement which led the Centre back to power in 1963.

The first notable achievement of the Right was to devalue the currency. This was done swiftly to the tune of almost 50 per cent and was one of the most successful operations of its kind in post-war European history. Devaluation hurt the working people, whose savings were in cash, but it proved a boon to the commercial classes. The import control system was abolished, and a major governmental worry as well as a source of corruption thus disappeared. Despite the huge devaluation, imports of consumer goods boomed.

Soon, distinct features of a new consumption pattern were to emerge: the better-off importing whatever they could, the urban poor and the peasantry providing the market for home industry. The demand pattern was strong enough to influence the supply; domestic industry exported practically none of its production. This naturally kept the balance of payments under strain. With an increasing trade deficit, Greece was becoming dependent on invisible earnings (of which shipping was traditional, while tourism and emigrants' remittances gradually provided important additions), on private capital inflow, and on foreign aid and loans. The latter two were practically under the control of the USA. No serious effort was made to control the dangerous growth of luxury imports by the higher income groups; the obsolete tariff was kept in being; and import-substitution was in practice rejected through the government's refusal to enter the private sector of the economy 'where the market is the best guide'.

In fact, it is tempting to see the worship of free enterprise as an economic counterpart to dogmatic anti-Communism. Apart from devaluation and free trade, the Right had no industrial or commercial policy at all. Bilateral agreements with the socialist bloc eventually became necessary for the disposal of agricultural products which were unmarketable elsewhere; but, despite their size, they were not discussed much and were seen as an unpleasant departure from an orderly neo-classical system. *Ad hoc* negotiations for the procurement of equipment in the West were seen as clever deals rather than as aids for a policy. Having renounced negative controls, the Right threw out proposals for imitating the Italian experiment in public enterprise, and for a planning mechanism in the French style, as tools for development. The private sector was crudely defined as anything in which money could be made, regardless of macro-economic implications or social policy. In the management of the economy, after the reconstruction phase was considered complete, the Right attempted to be somewhat Keynesian. But this was difficult, both for administrative reasons and, more, because the tax system was as a whole regressive. Ultimately, fiscal policy accentuated the fluctuations of economic activity. So far as there was any effective overall policy, it was confined to the use of monetary weapons.

Not unnaturally, the monetary authorities considered that their job was to guard against inflation. Restoring confidence in the currency, in fact, became the main slogan supporting what the Right meant by 'stability'. In this, the Central Bank was remarkably effective. The price level remained practically static, while private savings accumulated at rates impressive for the country's income level. Beyond combating inflation, however, the monetary authorities were entrusted with the job of encouraging productive and discouraging unproductive expenditure. But, despite much sophistication in the use of incentives and specifically of funds, the Bank succeeded neither in promoting overall private investment nor in channelling money away from the luxury import market, the gradually thriving housing boom or the straightforwardly illegal export of capital. In the words of X. Zolotas, who throughout this period was Governor of the Central Bank and architect of monetary policy:

> The expansion of credit to industry in 1957 and 1958 by *over four times* the rate of increase of industrial production showed that the commercial banks had not succeeded in their new role and were unable to prevent the *excessive* leakage of credit toward purposes *wholly unrelated* to industrial activity. (*Monetary Equilibrium and Economic Development*, p. 79; italics added)[1]

The reluctance of the private sector to invest in industry had deep-rooted causes. Lack of credit, as we have just seen, was not one of them. If anything it was the opposite – according to an OECD estimate, as much as 70 per cent of total private industrial assets were acquired from commercial bank loans. The lack of real and institutional infrastructure was not entirely imaginary but certainly a much exaggerated factor, particularly as public works were completed at a rapid rate. The real causes for the holding back of industry were more social and psychological than economic. Uncertainty, however imponderable, was perhaps of major importance in a country

1. The structure of investment is significant: in the twelve years between 1952 and 1963 out of a total fixed asset formation of 171,341 millions of drachmas (in current prices), 62,297 millions (36 per cent) were invested in housing, 24,912 millions (15 per cent) in agriculture, and only 22,049 millions (just over 700 million dollars) amounting to *only 13 per cent of total investment, in manufacturing*. While the percentage of gross national product invested in housing is probably the highest in Europe, fluctuating between 3·7 and 6·2 per cent, the investment in manufacture is certainly the lowest, never exceeding 2·3 per cent.

which had seen great vicissitudes. This was however more powerful in discouraging the small investor who, in any case, had one outlet besides a savings account – and that was housing. A stock market hardly existed, while the acquisition of shares belonging to family enterprises guaranteed no dividends whatever. The enterprises themselves, meanwhile, found solid industrial growth both more difficult and less remunerative than commerce or speculation. Efficiency, or rather the lack of it, was no barrier to survival, while the tariff, dating from the pre-war depression, was there to protect even steam-age technology. Family enterprises did not merge otherwise than by marriage. Industrial units were thus fragmented and had neither room for new products nor markets wide enough for new technologies. Growth, therefore, just kept up with the growth of incomes of those classes of the population who were consumers of domestic production. The beginnings of rationalization of obsolete technology and organization came only after association with the Common Market in 1961, which brought fears that protection must decline, while also bringing a modest influx of foreign industrial capital and therefore an element of competition.

At last, even the Right realized the extent of the private sector's reluctance to industrialize the country. Meanwhile, however, the government had moved into the economic field at a different level. Adamant though ministers were in keeping out of what was not the 'proper' role of the state, they grasped before it was too late that the infrastructure needed huge efforts and that there was no way of building it up other than by direct government investment. The expansion of public investment spending, despite its naïve single-mindedness and the corruption which was its inevitable by-product, was undoubtedly Karamanlis's historic decision – and a change radical enough to convince big sections of Liberal opinion that, at last, the Right was not purely destructive. True, economic development through road-building was only a partial view of the problem. But, given that the conservative state was incapable of doing anything more sophisticated, there is no doubt that public expenditure was one half of the 'engine of growth' which accounts for the remarkable growth-rates achieved in this period. Public investment expenditure rose from 1.7 billion drachmas in 1952 to 5.8 billion in 1962. The gross national product grew by an average of nearly 7 per cent a year in constant prices.

Naturally, it is not easy to assess how much of a contribution was made by public investment. By itself, it would certainly not have been enough to act as an engine of growth. But the missing half was provided by invisible exports. From 1957, tourism took on sizeable dimensions. Tourist receipts were soon growing at a rate of 20 per cent a year, with the further advantage that the money was shared in different regions and among different professions and classes. From 1956, emigration came into the picture too, though in a different manner. By 1960, 100,000 people were leaving Greece every year; and in 1963 their remittances amounted to $173 million. Finally, shipping – apart from providing jobs for the majority of the population from the islands – brought in $170 million of foreign exchange in 1963.

Foreign emigration may for a time have contributed to growth. On the other hand, it reflected two of the major problems which the type of economic growth achieved by the Right did not solve but rather accentuated. The first of these was inability to provide full employment. The second was inability to check the large and growing income inequalities. We have already seen that the industrial sector did not function as a spearhead. Its contribution to total employment, in fact, relatively and (by a small margin) absolutely diminished during the twelve years between 1952 and 1963. The service and parasitic sectors, although growing most rapidly, were still insufficient to keep up with population increase and particularly to provide stable and growing incomes. The growth of this tertiary sector was in any case a counterpart of the inability of other sectors to offer productive employment. The emigration to the towns and then abroad is inexplicable unless one considers the growing income inequalities between town and country. Underdeveloped agriculture could no longer satisfy the aspirations of the peasants: hence their migration for a better life to the towns or abroad, despite the fact that there too conditions were not easy or stable. The same 'demonstration effect' which accounts for the Europeanized consumption patterns of the higher income groups was at work throughout the social system.

Agriculture was still the largest sector of production. But the peasant world had substantially changed since the pre-war years. The resistance against the Germans, the civil war and the massive population movements that had then taken place had already increased the cultural interplay between town and country life. After the war these trends were intensified and the patterns of life of industrial society thus rapidly infiltrated the countryside. Roads brought tourists, while the spread of cinemas and transistor radios opened the peasants' eyes to the temptations of modern consumption. The vestiges of a closed and patriarchal socio-economic organization, first shattered by the short-lived EAM experiment, were now crumbling. The younger generation of peasants was gradually being pulled into the modern world.

But if the countryside was being opened up as never before, the inefficient structure of production on the land stayed the same. The main problems were still surplus peasant population, extremely low productivity, under-employment, monoculture in some regions, small and parcelled-out units, shortage of fertilizers and machines, and a system of exploitation based on the wholesalers paying miserly prices to the producers. The government did make some effort to tackle these problems. Crop policy was gradually readjusted, so that by 1958 Greece was self-sufficient in cereals. Sugar production was promoted and new export products – cotton, fresh fruit and vegetables, rice – were added to the traditional tobacco, currants and olive oil. Fertilizers were introduced on a large scale; the number of tractors, a mere 1,500 in 1940, reached 24,000 by 1962. Major attention was given to developing new crop land, and the arable area rose by 6 per cent in a decade. Public investment in agriculture represented over half the state's expenditure on capital account.

But the effort was misconceived. Despite the growth of

production and productivity, on the whole cultivation remained extensive. The large increases in cereal production disrupted the agrarian pattern of work and created a permanent strain on the Budget, which covered the gap between the cost of home production and the world price. It was so advantageous for producers and wholesalers alike that half the cultivated land was turned over to growing cereals. But the production of an export crop like cotton soon tailed off for lack of incentive, at the low prices secured by the growers of this labour-intensive crop. Thus, extensive cultivation was often import-substitution of the wrong kind, apart from the fact that it added to unemployment.

Also, the cost of agricultural growth was excessive. Public works, which were poorly planned and badly carried out, always exceeded their budget to the advantage of the private firms who did the job. However, output nearly doubled between 1952 and 1963.

While techniques changed, the institutional framework did not. The system of exploitation was not only preserved but strengthened. The bulk of products were taken to market through the traditional wholesaler channels. The strong co-operative movement which emerged in the 1950s was generally encouraged, but was kept firmly under the control of the party in power. An American anthropologist describes the government's attitude: 'Since the idea of pooling land sounded so much like a collective farm on the Communist model, the government carefully investigated to be sure no subversive influences were at work before it granted any loans' (I. T. Sanders, *Rainbow in the Rock*, p. 69). Thus, to the traditional wholesaler there were added the officially controlled councils of the cooperatives. Both stood between the individual farmer and the market, and they made up a powerful pressure group intimately linked with the Agricultural Bank and with the government's organization for winning elections. Through this grip on the peasants' livelihood, as we shall see, the Right was able to carry out its systematic policy of isolating them politically, ideologically and economically and thus keep them in leading-strings. This, in the last analysis, is what kept the Right 'constitutionally' in power.

Because of their harsh and dependent economic conditions, the peasants did not take any vigorous political action for a long time. The main effect of the plight of the countryside was not revolt but mass exodus to the towns. This in turn produced a problem of urban unemployment which, from 1955, took on alarming dimensions. A solution to this problem was found – outside the confines of the Greek economy. By this time, the post-war European boom had led to an acute shortage of labour. The advanced countries looked for workers from the underdeveloped south of Europe. Within ten years, 7 per cent of the population of Greece left the country temporarily or permanently. An estimate has been made of 600,000 emigrants for the period 1955–64. Though one cannot get an accurate total because there was so much clandestine emigration, and though one cannot distinguish between temporary and permanent departures, it is certain that from 1958 onwards net emigration was larger than the natural growth of the population. The mass of emigrants were younger people, presumably part of the enterprising section among the labour force. Later skilled labour joined the trek north: by 1961 49.6 per cent of emigrants were skilled. This climbed to 56.2 per cent for 1962. The long-term effects of the trend were clearly catastrophic, but it was encouraged by the Right, whose policies it suited well. The boiling pot of large unemployed masses was removed, domestic labour remained easy to control, the large remittances sent home by the emigrant workers helped the balance of payments and the economy's parasitic sector: the socio-economic structure may have weakened from the viewpoint of long-run prospects, but meantime it had strengthened the Right's social base.

Imports of foreign capital had long been considered by the Right as a stone to kill many birds. In the beginning of its rule they were seen mainly as a substitute assisting insufficient domestic finance. Later, and as US aid gradually diminished until it vanished, the emphasis was put on the balance of payments. Finally, as a domestic enterprise was nowhere to be seen, foreign capital became the panacea which would industrialize the country. By opening the gates to the country's 'protectors', the Right ensured that its further political and economic integration with NATO was achieved. The Right's policy fully corresponded to the interests of the economic oligarchy, whose main consideration was how to cling to their acquired advantages without any further risks. Imbued with the Common Market 'ideology' then developing, the oligarchy was looking forward to the time when Greece would be 'governed from Brussels', so that no Greek government of any complexion could interfere with their good life. Foreign capital was thus more than welcomed. If the choice of heavy reliance on foreign capital was ultimately incompatible with a survival of economic and political national independence (a fact that was to become all too obvious in later years), it permitted the Right to hope that an almost immovable and self-strengthening social structure, fully corresponding to their interests, could be made permanent. The rapid rise in urban incomes could proceed so long as foreign capital and remittances from abroad continued to pour in, thus cementing a social balance rightly considered as still precarious for them. By the time income inequalities produced dangerous social tensions, it was felt that Greece would be so inextricably integrated in the US block that her ruling class would be beyond danger.

The opening of the Greek economy to foreign private capital was made official in 1953, through a law offering prospective investors special tax exemptions, freedom to re-export capital plus interest and profits, as well as numerous other facilities. But, though the advantages offered were extraordinary, the amount of foreign capital actually invested was not significant until 1960. Between 1954 and 1964 investments of 450 million dollars had been approved by the government, but of this only 170 millions had actually entered the country. About 40 per cent of this inflow was American-owned, a fact which marks the first noteworthy penetration of US finance in the Greek economy. If the figures do not seem impressive, they bear comparison with total capital assets in Greek manufacturing. According to estimates presented by the ERE Minister of Coordination in 1962, the total of post-war domestic manufacturing investment amounted to 632 million dollars, out of which a mere 220 millions belonged to the largest 447 firms. Thus foreign investment actually carried out by 1964 almost equalled the total assets of the manufacturing sector proper. Their power was, however, incommensurably greater because of the much larger units established.

An example makes the process clear. In 1962 the powerful ESSO corporation undertook to invest 110 million dollars, later increased to 190 millions, to set up a large industrial complex near Salonica, including a petroleum refinery, a steel plant and a petrochemical complex. By the time the project was nearing completion, Pappas, the Greek–American magnate who is in charge, controlled between one-fifth and one-sixth of total Greek manufacturing capacity.

Not surprisingly, the shifts introduced in the control of economic decision-taking further modified the structure of political power. The pre-war economic penetration by mainly British capital operated largely through the Greek power system, thus creating stable alliances which had long-term interests in the country's economic future. Foreign investment since the war remained, by contrast, largely independent of domestic economic interests. Hence its tie with the country was directly through its links with the government, a fact which inevitably led to an alliance with the governing party.

The Right claimed to have achieved a 'Greek economic miracle'. The claim is only partly justified. Regardless of the fact that the international economic environment was favourable, regardless of the opportunities that were lost, and equally regardless of the economic mistakes or the social cost of achieving the end, it remains true that when the Right fell from power, national income per head of the population exceeded 400 US dollars. Though not yet rich, Greece was no longer a poor country.

This does not mean, however, that the country had been put on the road to economic development. Even apart from the fact that the Right was producing a growingly inegalitarian and unjust society, on purely technical grounds their economic policy must be found wanting: they did not succeed in creating employment opportunities so that Greeks might live in their own country.

CHAPTER 10

Conservative Supremacy – Political (1952–63)

THE political counterpart of the socio-economic structure evolved in these years is closely related to the maintenance of political 'stability', which was inaugurated when Papagos's 'Greek Rally' came to power in 1952. For if the promise of political and economic stabilization greatly contributed to the assumption of power by the Right, it could hardly suffice for an indefinite maintenance of a sufficiently large and solid social and political basis. The impact of anti-Communist propaganda would necessarily lose its grip, and the force of events would inevitably exercise a strong pressure towards more radical solutions incompatible with the maintenance of the oligarchy's privileges. New popular forces would emerge challenging the foundations of the system. The established rules of the parliamentary system would eventually undermine what the Right was there to preserve. However, for twelve years (1952–63) the party in office ruled unperturbed, enjoying ample parliamentary majorities, its popular vote varying between 42 and 51 per cent.[1]

But although the maintenance of the Right in power was periodically endorsed by popular vote, parliamentary representation did not correspond to the true balance of forces. It was the majority electoral system imposed by the US that had brought Papagos to power in 1952. Similarly, it was through able manipulation of electoral systems, elaborated *ad hoc*

1. A table showing the percentage of votes and seats in Parliament respectively by the main political formations is highly significant.

	1952	1956	1958	1961
Right	49·22 % (82 %)	47·38 % (55 %)	41·17 % (57 %)	50·81 % (59 %)
Centre	34·22 % (17 %)	} 48·15 % (44 %) (Centre and Left)	20·68 % (12 %)	33·66 % (33·5 %)
			10·62 % (3 %)	
Left	9·55 % (–)		24·33 % (26·5 %)	14·63 % (8 %)

before each general election, that the 'Greek Rally' and subsequently the ERE, as it was renamed by Karamanlis, managed to swell their representation in Parliament and keep themselves in power. The deliberate refusal to readjust the electoral lists according to the new (1951) population census resulted in grave disproportions of representation between the urban centres, where the Centre and Left were stronger, and the agrarian regions where the Right was powerful. In 1958 for example, in Athens, where the ERE percentage was 29 per cent, 23,244 votes corresponded to one seat. In Thesprotia (Epirus) where the predominance of the Right was enormous (57.8 per cent) it only needed 6,862 votes to elect one deputy. In the seven most over-represented electoral regions ERE was stronger than average in all but one case.

In 1956 the coalition opposed to ERE won more votes than ERE but only obtained 44 per cent of the seats in Parliament against 56 per cent of the party in power. In the next elections (1958) an elaborate system of penalization of coalitions was put forward, which impeded the grouping of anti-governmental forces. Thus the number of ERE deputies rose from 165 to 171 while their votes dwindled from 47.38 per cent to 41.17 per cent. In 1961, the electoral system became even more complicated: while retaining the majority system in the provinces (still on the basis of the completely antiquated 1940 census, despite the availability of another census that had taken place in March of that year) proportional representation was the method used in the urban centres.

However, the results of the 1961 elections were bitterly challenged by the opposition forces. The electoral manipulations were denounced and the whole system of electoral fraud was exposed. For this time it was not only the electoral system that had been manipulated in the government's interests. Down to the smallest details, the party in power had organized an elaborate system that resulted in blunt misrepresentation. Military votes, overwhelmingly for the ERE, were organized on separate lists under military control. Illegal entries in the electoral lists enabling double or multiple voting were exposed on a large scale. The numbers of double voters were enormous: numbers up to 500,000 have been put forward. Even if one allows for gross exaggeration due to the heated political controversy, it cannot be doubted that ERE was thus strengthened with a considerable number of non-existent voters.

Besides fraud, the 1961 elections were also marked by violence. The system of electoral misrepresentation was complemented by the systematic oppression practised in the countryside, especially during electoral campaigns. Potential left-wing and Centre voters were all known in country localities and in the smaller electoral polling stations (wards) of smaller towns; this made a subsequent check on the votes cast comparatively easy. Pro-governmental ballot sheets with distinctive signs were distributed, and their recipients were threatened with sanctions were the sheet not to be found in the poll. A small number of sheets were subsequently actually checked, a fact which added to the credibility of the general threats. Moreover, the actual methods practised in order to implement threats against political dissension were extremely efficient. The chronic dependence of the great majority of the peasantry on loans by the government-controlled Agricultural Bank, or for the repeatedly needed moratoria for the repayment of debts, had gradually led to a considerable economic dependence of the individual farmer on the state. This dependence was further accentuated by the local gendarmerie's authority to impose large fines or to charge the villagers with real or imaginary minor offences. Offences like not keeping the dog leashed, not keeping the garden clean or not having whitewashed the walls were prosecuted on the criterion of whether or not the peasant was politically docile. The inordinately high fines and expenses thereby imposed made the economic survival of the peasant strictly dependant on the representative of the central authority, that is, on the gendarme's good will.

Economic oppression affected not only the individual but also the community through the mechanisms of local administration:

> The Community council does not maintain law and order, does not have much to say about local schools. Even in those affairs where it is supposed to have jurisdiction, such as drawing up its own budget or

arranging for the collection of taxes, it has to gain the approval of the Nomarch [equivalent of the French prefect] who is appointed by the Ministry of Interior. (Sanders, p. 229)

Approval was given on the basis of purely political criteria: 'Such and such a thing becomes impossible, because the village had not voted for the party in power.' (ibid., p. 238)

Economic pressure was combined with positive oppression. Right-wing bands aided the gendarmerie and a special body of Civil Guards (TEA) was built up originally along the frontiers but subsequently all over the country. TEA's role in terrorizing the peasants was enormous. Carrying arms at any time, they beat up opponents, raided the countryside and occasionally burned down farms and crops of dissidents. They constituted a permanent barrier to any ideological penetration of Left or even mildly anti-governmental propaganda. Left-wing newspapers did not even circulate in the provinces and even Centre ones were bought and read at a certain risk. The radio stations were synonymous with party propaganda. In the frontier regions, tension was permanently maintained. Special authorization (characteristically issued not by the political authorities but by the Army) was necessary for non-residents to enter the region, and even members of Parliament or candidates of the Left, and sometimes of the Centre, were refused the right to enter even during their electoral campaigns.

Revealing of the pressure effectively used are the electoral results in the border regions. In 1958 ERE won between 71 per cent and 86 per cent of the votes, and in 1961 when the oppression reached its maximum the percentage rose to between 91 per cent and 100 per cent.

The situation in the village Litochoron as reported by the French newspaper *Le Monde* depicts the prevailing atmosphere. On 10 October 1961, the military commander of the TEA assembled the population at the gendarmerie station and urged them to kill the candidates of the Left, were they to appear in the village. Two days later, on 12 October, twenty men under the leadership of an officer in uniform seriously injured a left-wing candidate and four peasants. When the intervention of the regional administrative chief (the Nomarch) was solicited, he refused on the grounds that he could not intervene for fear of falsifying the free play of the system!

The oppression, which never ceased in the countryside, was not, however, sufficient to maintain the Right in power. Even though the rapid rise in incomes of the middle classes and the expansion of the parasitic tertiary sector had created a larger social base than the Right previously disposed of, the alliance between upper and lower middle classes was not broad enough for the Right to be indifferent to the free interplay of social forces which would inevitably result in the shattering of the propaganda system that had been based on the civil war. Further, the alliance itself was precarious, to the extent that its maintenance depended on the continuation of the economic boom that had enabled the middle classes to grow.

It is thus easy to explain why the special measures taken during the civil war were never abolished. The Communist Party was still outlawed and administrative deportation was maintained. Apart from those still kept in prison on the basis of an ordinary conviction (in 1962 there were still 1,350 political prisoners), thousands of persons were detained in concentration camps in the islands of Agios Efstratios and Yaros until almost the end of the Karamanlis administration. The camps, and the nightmare island of Makronissos where hundreds of thousands of young men of left-wing ideas or suspected of such, were interned under the pretext of military conscription, served not only to neutralize all potential opponents, but also to intensify the disarray of what was left of the Communist movement. Torture, isolation and blackmail were used in order to extract written statements disavowing Communism. The then Minister of Defence, Panayiotis Kanellopoulos, referred to this operation as 'building the new Parthenon'. The strict 'no signature' line of the Communist Party led to the implicit or explicit condemnation of all those who succumbed to torture, as stooges, traitors or simply 'unworthy of the party', and consequently to the political isolation of vast numbers who had given in. The neutralization and subsequent depoliticization of innumerable militants that resulted from this practice, as well as the refusal of the government to allow the repatriation of over 80,000 Greeks who had taken refuge in the socialist countries after the end of the civil war, deprived the Left of the majority of their old effectives.

The political and ideological neutralization of the organized Left was, however, not enough. Repression in the large towns was taking new forms designed to contain the labour movement. While open terrorism had become, especially after 1955, far less conspicuous, the machinery of pressure remained constant. A 'certificate of national probity' was required as a condition for things as diverse as being employed by the state or by any private or semi-public firm controlled by the state, obtaining a driver's licence or a passport, getting into the University, hunting or fishing, and innumerable other everyday activities requiring for one reason or another an administrative authorization. The result was a suffocating atmosphere. In a country where unemployment was, at least until the mass emigration of the late fifties, the most urgent problem for the majority of the people, the threat of not being able to find a job was probably the most effective method of political control. Elaborate lists of 'non-nationalists' were kept by the police, on the basis of which the certificate was refused. Although the accurate number of persons on this black list is unknown, it has been estimated to be in the order of 1,000,000.

The control of trade unions by the government added to the oppression of the working class. Since 1946, when Tsaldaris had sacked the trade union leadership and had imposed his own men, mostly remnants of the Metaxist guilds, the workers had never managed to overcome the institutional obstructions that made genuine representation impossible. Though trade unionism was in principle free, an elaborate system of representation was organized to exclude the posibility of a radical labour leadership. Each union, regardless of the number of its adherents, elected one representative to the General Confederation. Dwarf unions of ten members were 'constructed' and could counterbalance a union with thousands of members, thus dominating the whole structure of the

Confederation, which became the 'official' labour union to which all workers were obliged to pay a significant fraction of their wages. The anti-labour policy of the 'General Confederation', combined with continuous pressure on the part of the state and employers who threatened genuine representatives as well as union members with dismissal and persecution, contributed to the corruption and underdevelopment of the labour movement. By 1963 over one half of the workers were not organized at all.

The official attitude towards strikes was even harder. Although the Constitution recognized strikes as a right of the worker, a Metaxist law giving the government the authority of 'political conscription' of strikers was often applied, thereby transforming the continuation of the strike into a criminal offence. The same effect resulted from another law passed in 1955, which forbade strikes after the Ministry of Labour had offered to mediate between employers and strikers. In any case, the police did not hesitate to intervene brutally whenever popular demonstrations assumed any dimensions. Demonstrations of workers were in general those repressed most systematically.

In short the actual institutional framework operating during this period was in flagrant opposition to the Constitution. If from a purely judicial point of view, the operation of the system was legal, since it depended on a legally promulgated set of norms, it must be stressed that its establishment had taken place during the civil war, when 'exceptional' legislation could find justification in the spirit if not the letter of the Constitution. Its maintenance, however, throughout the fifties, when the 'exceptional' circumstances had long ceased and there was absolutely no danger of any kind, internal or external, had as its main objective to keep the Right in office, against not only the Communists, who were militarily defeated, morally broken and politically isolated, but against all social forces that might even threaten its monopoly of political power.

The 'legal' institutional framework, referred to by Greeks as the para-constitution, was by itself not enough to ensure a permanent right-wing dominance. A large mechanism of coercion had to operate in order actually to carry out the political, economic and police measures of oppression. This coercion apparatus, which would function on the fringes of institutionalized para-legality, was already in place. Instead of dismantling what they inherited from Metaxas, the Nazis and the civil war, the Right strengthened it: police, gendarmerie, civil guard and intelligence agencies took on extraordinary dimensions. Enormous sums, never listed in the ordinary budgets and free from any kind of control, were credited to the security services who, according to one estimate, had by 1962 over 60,000 persons on their secret payroll.

Thus, the existence of the Constitution and the parliamentary system did not prevent the growth and consolidation of a parallel centre of sovereign authority and power. The role of the armed forces within this 'parallel' state was extremely important. While consuming between 40 and 50 per cent of the ordinary budget, a fact which is partly explained by constant American and NATO pressure, they were both financially and organizationally almost totally uncontrolled by the political authorities. Though their fundamental outlook was indistinguishable from that of the party in power, whom they supported politically with all their might, the military never consented to relinquish their semi-autonomous status which was first built up by the British in 1943–4.

The real force within the Army was a secret society called 'IDEA', created in the Middle East in October 1944. This secret society controlled the Army and ensured its ideological homogeneity. As the 'ultimate guarantee' for the protection of the social order, IDEA held even the mildest proposal for reform to be a dangerous subversive activity. The structure of the Army was such that anti-Communist hysteria found good soil to grow in. Bad payment of regular officers, professional frustration and insufficient integration in society were the counterpart of the puffing-up of their own importance as guardians of the cultural, religious and historical quintessence of the 'Nation'.

For example: a letter from General Gogousis, reputed to

be among the leaders of IDEA, was brought to light in 1950. In this letter he admonished the organization to create a special service to 'assassinate anyone who harmed the struggle and betrayed the fatherland'. This almost messianic faith in the symbols which the army was 'there to protect' was rooted in the fanatical puritanism of the petty-bourgeois environment which most of the officers came from. Throughout the decade the officer corps stewed in their own juice, pressing for more and more credits to 'fight the Cold War' and deter 'the internal enemy'. Their position had been strengthened after the incorporation of Greece in NATO and the war in Korea. A state within the state, running their own secret services and intelligence agencies, the armed forces were increasingly independent even of the political Right. The blatant intervention of the armed forces in the 1961 election was the culmination of a long process in which the Army became increasingly autonomous. It was their first *open* participation in the political scene since the end of the civil war. (Excepting an alleged attempt of a *coup* suppressed by Papagos in 1951, and supposedly provoked by the Marshal's decision to resign from the Army and enter politics. However, there is no certifiable evidence on this.) The alleged fact that their intervention was put into effect against the will of Karamanlis is characteristic of a growing intolerance of the Right's 'mistakes'. The direct offspring of this mentality is the 21 April 1967 *coup d'état*. However, as long as there was a fundamental agreement on the aims to be pursued, there was full collaboration in containing the common enemy.

In short, through the institutionalization of a series of repressive standards, and the organization of an elaborate system of coercion, the Right had created the conditions for a perpetuation of its political monopoly. Eventually, however, the very process through which the democratic structures had been atrophied resulted in the centres of decision moving away from the political world. The open intervention of the King in the designation of Karamanlis as Papagos's successor to the premiership contributed to the failure to work out a democratic party structure for the Right. Karamanlis, like his predecessor, reigned as an absolute dictator within his party, backed by the forces that had put him in place.

Following the pre-war pattern, the party as a more or less coherent organization had only two functioning elements: the leader himself, surrounded by his 'inner circle' of advisers, and the parliamentary group of deputies. The position of the latter, however, had been considerably weakened because of the incommensurably greater scope and power of the state mechanism. Party politics and propaganda were not pursued through the organs provided for in the party statutes (which did not really exist), but directly through the state, whose mechanism, at least at the higher levels, was fully identified with the party. Thus, instead of being authors of responsible political decision-making, the deputies and even to a certain extent the members of the cabinet (a senior minister of the Karamanlis government resigned in 1959 because he did not manage to see the Prime Minister for eight months), found themselves absolutely dependent on the Prime Minister, who alone decided on policy and distributed credits and patronage.

The dependence of deputies on the Prime Minister is explained if one examines the mode of representation. The system of political 'clientelism' had been re-established, so that it was local notables who ensured the communication of the electorate with its representatives. The deputies' social and political role was still centred on meeting the voters' needs. Given the degree of under-development, the possibility of satisfying these needs concretely was of paramount importance. Whether the request was to find a job, to be admitted to hospital free of charge, to ensure a loan or to be given a state contract; or to put pressure for the carrying out of minor or major investments or public works in the electoral district: the fulfilment of the clientèle's needs, upon which the re-election of the representative depended, was in the hands of the Premier and the state machine which he controlled. Thus the role of Parliament gradually degenerated into a lobby for the promotion of individual or specific group interests. The tedious methods used to camouflage this process went to the extreme of tacking 'personal' clauses, granting advantages to persons or groups, on to totally irrelevant legal statutes. A new sport developed in Athens, which was to search for the 'Who's Who' in each new law and decree.

But if it was the Premier and his inner circle who were the operational agents of state policy, they themselves were dependent on the network of vested interests which kept Karamanlis in power. Having risen to his post by royal favour, Karamanlis was only superficially the boss. The very degeneration of the parliamentary system, for which his authoritarian method of government was heavily to blame, had in turn deprived him of a solid constitutional foundation on which to base the government's independence of the extra-parliamentary Establishment. For, beyond Parliament and the government, the all too real centres of power were the Army, the Palace, a small circle of politicians and civil servants, and a number of bankers, industrialists and shipowners. The close relationship between political and economic oligarchy is revealed by the fact that the half-dozen biggest political 'names' had personal or family connexions with big business, military circles and figures of the Court.

In addition to its strictly political role, which can hardly be exaggerated in this period, the Palace was directly and indirectly involved in economic affairs to the degree that it was in itself part of big business. Its exact role is difficult to establish because of the extreme secrecy surrounding royal economic activities. But, in addition to the exorbitant sums received officially by the King (in 1964, $650,000 a year), he – or rather Queen Frederika – was entrusted with managing the so-called 'Queen's Fund', through which an estimated $10 million of public funds were used by the Palace to promote a number of worthy objectives, totally uncontrolled by the state. To what extent the Palace took part in other, more dubious financial activities through the transmission-belt of the group of bankers, shipowners and industrialists known as the 'Royal clan', we cannot ascertain. What is certain, however, is that – whatever the exact relationships – there was hardly a significant sector of public life free from the ultimate control of what has been called 'the closed politics of the Royal clan'. Prime Minister, Party, Army and economic oligarchy looked to the King as their sovereign and protector, (See J. Meynaud, *Les Forces politiques en Grèce,* p. 338.) If it were possible to speak of any single centre of power, we should have to look for it within the Palace walls. Gradually, crowned democracy was slipping back to the nineteenth-century model: constitutional – or unconstitutional? – monarchy.

CHAPTER 11

Foreign Powers and the Cyprus Problem (1952–64)

THE Truman Doctrine marked Greece's entry into the American orbit. But it was only when Greece was admitted to NATO in 1952 that this alignment found its definite consolidation. Yet the latter was the necessary result of the former. If Greece's foreign policy could, under other circumstances, have been oriented either toward her immediate Balkan neighbours, or toward the countries of the Middle East, the domestic results of the civil war in combination with the international cold war setting on the one hand, and the economic dependence on the US on the other, left no actual choice. Seen in its historical context, the decision to enter NATO was an inescapable necessity. The possibility (whether real or fictitious) of another Communist bid for power made the need for integration within a larger and more comprehensive power bloc the cornerstone of Greek foreign policy. And it was only because Britain opposed her entry at the time that Greece was not a founding member of NATO. Indeed, Britain tried for a period to stop Greece and Turkey from entering NATO, with the object of creating a similar defence organization in the Eastern Mediterranean in which she would have the upper hand. But, inevitably, the brief Anglo-American rivalry, whose repercussions on Greek domestic policy we have already seen, ended with Britain's defeat. In August 1951 Greece applied for admission and on 18 February 1952 she was, together with Turkey, admitted to NATO.

But this event had results that were totally unforeseen by the Greek politicians and particularly the Centre, who were in office when the treaty was negotiated and signed. (It is interesting to recall this fact in the light of subsequent accusations by the Right that the Centre was crypto-Communist.) Joining NATO was seen as a panacea for the most crucial national problems, so the terms and implications of admission were not even discussed. So great was the eagerness of almost all Greek politicians to accept the gift from heaven, and so deep their fear of offending their allies by pondering over the terms, that, as a painstaking analysis of the parliamentary debates shows, Greece entered NATO without really knowing what to expect in terms of obligations (Theodore A. Kouloumbis, *Greek Political Reaction to American and NATO Influences*, p. 49) For NATO did much more than protect the country from external aggression: it also provided the context within which US influence would be kept constantly active. Up to the integration of the Greek army in NATO, the decisive American power over the Army was justified by the extraordinary circumstances that prevailed during and immediately after the civil war. The normalization of the situation would, however, lead to limiting US influence to the 'normal' diplomatic and economic channels. NATO functioned both as the institutional framework and as the organizational instrument for the maintenance of a permanent network for the preservation of US control. Many years were, however, to elapse before the full implications of the institutionalization of US presence became manifest. For the time being the Americans were the unanimously acclaimed saviours of the country. The curtailment of national independence was, of course, foreseen and accepted. Papagos stated it bluntly in 1952:

> When we exist not only thanks to our own decision, but because the Americans exist, and they report to their citizens, under what type of logic can we deny them the right to have their own opinions? . . . We must understand that we are members of a family of nations, and this creates a new reality . . . . We will see that many things, exceptional according to theory, have become already rules of our public life.

and Papandreou's position was hardly different:

> Those who think that we can live in the current face of the world with the old understanding of sovereignty are wrong. But as it is certain that the period of independence has passed, it is equally certain that the period of subjugation applies only to the iron curtain and not to the free peoples.

We have already seen the fundamental role played by the

US in the fall of the liberal Plastiras government and the coming to power of Papagos's Greek Rally. Given such an unconditionally friendly government, the US could afford to be far less blatant in its interventions. Thus, the agreement which gave the US Army free use of Greek territory was signed in a very hush-hush way, while the King was absent and Parliament was not in session. Under pressure, Foreign Minister Stephanopoulos admitted in Parliament (25 November 1953) that the agreement, signed on 12 October, was reached under the threat that if Greece refused to ratify it she would be expelled from NATO. But there was hardly any protest, so far as the essence of the agreement went. Greece was offering the US unrestricted use of roads, railways and areas needed for military purposes and was granting the right of uncontrolled entry, exit, movement and use of Greek territory to all American personnel. US activities were exempted from any taxation or charge; and the US could claim all kinds of services at rates 'not exceeding those paid by the Greek armed forces' – that is to say, usually nothing. All installations and equipment were freely removable, and the Greek government undertook to compensate the Americans for anything they might choose to leave behind. Finally, the military and civilian US functionaries, as well as their families, were granted extraterritorial rights – that is, immunity from the jurisdiction of Greek civil and criminal courts.

The signature of the Balkan Pact between Greece, Yugoslavia and Turkey in August 1954 seemed to set the seal on the ambitions of Greek foreign policy. Firmly entrenched in the Western alliance, Greece was entering on a course of full collaboration with her neighbours, where this was not incompatible with the continuing cold war. Moreover, Yugoslavia ceased to make any claims about the rights of a separate Macedonian nation. Greek territorial claims against Albania concerning northern Epirus – even though the state of war started in 1940 had not been formally terminated, and indeed still hasn't – were not meant very seriously. It was for the sake of appearances more than for reasons of substance that they were periodically put forward.

Thus, there was apparently nothing to threaten the almost bucolic unanimity – always with the exception of the totally powerless Left – that reigned over foreign policy issues, until the problem of self-determination for Cyprus arose. Out of the blue, the Cypriot problem successively burst the Balkan Pact, threatened the south-eastern flank of NATO with total demolition, almost provoked war three times between Greece and Turkey, and finally contributed in a big way to the abolition of democracy in Greece. For almost fifteen years, it has been the nightmare of Greek politicians, whether in office or in opposition.

It all started back in 1878. Under the Treaty of Berlin, the island was ceded by the Sultan to Britain after 400 years of Turkish rule, which had not, however, altered the predominantly Greek character of the population. In 1881 Cyprus was inhabited by 137,631 Greeks and 45,458 Turks – a ratio of three to one. Naturally enough, the Greek population saw British administration as a prelude to unification with Greece. This was, it was thought, only a matter of time. Britain was sure to repeat the gesture that had led to the return of the Ionian islands to Greece. When Churchill visited the island in 1907, he saluted the will of the Cypriot people to become an integral part of their mother-country. 'Such sentiments,' he said, 'are a proof of the patriotic attachment which nobly distinguishes the Greek people.'

Cyprus was in fact offered to Greece in 1915, when Greek entry into the war on the Allied side was considered to be of prime importance. King Constantine, however, was not enticed and the offer was buried. Two years later, when Venizelos's revolution brought Greece into the war, not a word was mentioned about Cyprus. The end of the First World War consolidated the situation. First in Sèvres (1920) and then in Lausanne (1923) Turkey abandoned all her claims on the island, which was formally annexed by Britain, and in 1925 became a Crown colony.

Thus to the Cypriots the hope of unification with Greece remained as remote as ever. Agitation gradually spread among the Greek-speaking community, culminating in the serious troubles that took place in 1941. The widespread popular demonstrations gave birth to the slogan of Enosis – union with Greece. But these were savagely repressed by the British authorities, while the Greek Prime Minister, Venizelos, permanently aligned towards an unconditional acceptance of British wishes, refused to support the Cypriot cause. Without support from Greece and with the international situation rapidly deteriorating, agitation gradually subsided. When, however, the Second World War started, the Cypriots were encouraged to fight for Britain, the insinuation being that the hour of unification with Greece was now approaching. Consequently, Greek flags that had been carefully hidden for fear of oppression were hoisted on the masts, and 30,000 Cypriots volunteered and distinguished themselves on the Allied side.

After victory had been attained, and for eight more years, the Cypriots waited for what they considered as the natural crowning of their efforts. A plebiscite organized in 1950 left no doubt as to the population's will: 96 per cent of the Greeks and 79 per cent of the island's total adult population voted for Enosis. But the Greek governments were hardly cooperative. Already in 1946, Prime Minister Tsaldaris had declared that 'the question of Cyprus is not a demand and it should not be posed in a vindictive manner; it only concerns Greece and her friend Great Britain.' He could have been speaking for his successors too. As long as British influence in Greece was preponderant there could be no question of international pressure. It is no coincidence that the first Greek Premier who dared to defy the British was Papagos, whose rise to power had been largely due to the US victory in the silent Anglo-American rivalry for Greece. It is true that the British had given him good reasons to break the chronic truce. In 1954, one year after renewed agitation under the inspired leadership of Archbishop Makarios had brought the Cyprus problem to the UN, the British Under-Secretary for Colonial Affairs, Hopkinson, found it opportune to declare, referring to Cyprus, that 'certain Commonwealth territories can *never* hope to reach full independence'. For, as Macmillan is reported to have said, 'Cyprus, hm ... how did Disraeli describe it to Queen Victoria? The key to Western Asia' (Charles Foley, *Legacy of Strife*, p. 16.). These were the days when Britain was retreating from her more exposed position in Suez. As Eden put the matter:

> In geography and in tactical considerations, the Turks have the stronger claim on Cyprus; in race and language the Greeks; in strategy the British, so long as their industrial life depends on oil supplies from the Persian Gulf. (*Full Circle*, p. 315)

This in a nutshell was the logic behind British strategy in the attempt to preserve Cyprus as a colony.

Thus, when Papagos, who then believed he could once more count on US support, decided to back the Cypriot cause, and brought the case before the General Assembly of the United Nations, Britain decided that the dormant Turkish element in Cyprus might prove to be useful in fighting the Greek claim. All Turkish rights had lapsed since the end of the First World War, and throughout the inter-war agitation the Turkish minority, which had by then dwindled from one-fourth to approximately one-fifth of the population, had not been at all present in the political arena. Full harmony prevailed between the two communities, and there was no more question of the Turkish minority imposing a veto on the wishes of the majority than there had been in the case of Rhodes, which was returned to Greece in 1947, and was both nearer the Turkish mainland and contained a larger percentage of Turks. As C. M. Woodhouse has pointed out, 'the British seemed to argue the Turkish case before the Turks ever thought of it' (*The Story of Greece*, p. 271). For approximately fifty years, during which the demand of the Cypriots for self-determination had been manifesting itself in various forms, it had never occurred to the Turks to put up an argument; they did not in fact enter the picture as long as the categorical British refusal to accept any discussion kept the demand for self-determination on the level of academic discourse.

The invitation to Turkey to join in was naturally not turned down by the Turkish government. They saw a chance to shift public opinion in Turkey away from burning domestic issues.

The Cyprus imbroglio was thus transformed from a typical struggle of colonized versus colonialists into a major international problem involving, apart from the Cypriot people themselves, three European countries, all members of NATO. Macmillan was soon to shrug his shoulders and say: 'Why do they hold Cyprus against us? It was nothing but a quarrel between Greeks and Turks and we settled it' (Foley, p. 149).

In April 1955, the Greek Cypriots, disillusioned with the possibilities of a peaceful solution, started an armed struggle in order to make their presence better felt. EOKA, as the clandestine resistance organization was called, rapidly dominated the island. Under the leadership of the experienced Colonel Grivas of 'X' fame, and with the Archbishop's blessing, the peaceful island became a hell of violence. The British had to face a dilemma: either they had to give in and accept some kind of compromise, or they would have to proceed to a long and violent suppression of a movement which was backed by practically the whole of the island's population. A conference was called in August 1955 between the British, Greek and Turkish governments, in which the Cypriots were unrepresented. The conference, however, ended in disaster. Turkey's Premier, Adnan Menderes, 'manufactured' the bombing of a Turkish mosque in Salonica, and then organized the Istanbul mobs in terrible retaliatory assaults against the Greek population. Menderes's role in organizing the violent incidents was established during his subsequent trial by the Turkish military who had him hanged – on different charges. At the time, however, the incident had far-reaching effects. Apart from breaking Greco–Turkish friendship, public opinion in Turkey had become sufficiently aroused to preclude any solution not conforming to Turkey's newly defined interests. And Turkish public opinion was important for NATO's internal stability, even more important than that of Greece. Very ably, Menderes had imposed himself as a permanent partner of Britain in the Cyprus problem. Britain had brought him in, but she could not get him out, or persuade him to any moderate solution. He played his part only too well. A referee was needed to adjudicate between the conflicting demands of Greece and Turkey and the good offices of the British government were offered, but all the conversations and negotiations that followed necessarily failed: self-determination, which would automatically lead to ENOSIS, could not even be discussed, even as a remote eventuality. Britain had found a way of permanently maintaining her bases. For with ENOSIS ruled out, all other solutions could be kept under her control.

Throughout 1955 and 1956 EOKA's struggle was intensified. Despite violent repression and the deportation of Archbishop Makarios to the Seychelles, the Cypriot resistance could not be broken. All British plans for some type of self-government under British authority were turned down by the Greeks. For the pressure of Greek domestic opinion had become in the meantime extremely strong. In the fall of 1955 (after the violent incidents in Istanbul) the NATO countries unanimously voted against Greece in the UN General Assembly. Uproar consequently reached its climax. Anti-American and anti-British feelings were virtually universal and for the first time the allegiance of Greece to NATO was put to question. Even the Right felt extremely uneasy. Though the government never raised the question openly, the most authoritative right-wing newspaper unequivocally attacked the US and Great Britain, advocated an isolationist foreign policy of strict neutrality and stated that 'We do not know what the government wants. But the people want withdrawal from NATO' (*Kathimerini*, 22 September 1955). Two weeks later, Papagos died. The unforeseen designation of Karamanlis as his successor should be seen in the light of the strong US pressure to put an end to the explosive situation. King Paul was obviously going beyond his authority by choosing Karamanlis for the job, but though the new Premier's accession was followed by an unmistakable shift towards conciliatory positions, public opinion was so aroused that any compromise excluding ENOSIS risked provoking chain-reactions of unpredictable amplitude. Thus if the new Premier made haste to proclaim the country's unquestioned allegiance to NATO and the usefulness of Greco–Turkish friendship, he did not dare to dissociate himself from an uncompromising ENOSIS line. When the British proposed the so-called Radcliffe Constitution (1957), granting full autonomy except for defence and foreign policy, it was unequivocably rejected.

It was then that the British committed a serious blunder which complicated the issue beyond their control. In order to blackmail Greece into accepting the compromise, Lennox Boyd threatened the partition of the island as an alternative solution. However, because of the complete geographical integration of the two communities, partition was entirely impracticable: half the inhabitants of the island would have to be forcibly moved, with catastrophic social and economic results. But the bait was eagerly snatched by the Turks. From now on, whenever Greek pressure mounted, the Turkish government threatened to take their own part, by force if needed. NATO threatened to disintegrate. The Turks, whom Britain had brought in to balance the Greeks, were now creating a serious problem for the United States, who were obliged to become involved as arbitrators.

With EOKA violence intensifying and the relations between the two Cypriot communities rapidly deteriorating, the situation had by 1957 become internationally explosive. The release of Makarios, and the replacement of the uncompromisingly hard Field-Marshal Harding by the more agile and liberal Sir Hugh Foot, did not do much to improve matters. When a series of violent incidents between Cypriot Greeks and Turks in July 1958 resulted in the two home countries being for some weeks on the verge of war, the Americans were seriously concerned. Much more than the maintenance of the British bases seemed to be at stake. The south-eastern flank of NATO was no longer operational and the tension between Turkey and Greece could spread no one knew how far, particularly if the Soviet Union saw fit to exploit the situation. Consequently, a way out had to be found at any cost and very heavy pressure was put on the Greek government to accept a non-Enosis solution. This now appeared feasible. Karamanlis was more firmly entrenched; he had just won the election of 1958 and could afford to face some internal discontent. Besides, public opinion was showing signs of lassitude. The threat of war with Turkey, some months earlier, had caused second thoughts among some of the intransigent elements who had supported the Cypriot demand for immediate self-determination. Complete independence for Cyprus – but to the exclusion of Enosis – was offered instead. Makarios, who was thus in effect appointed chief of a new state, could not put up a decisive resistance against pressure and temptation.

In the absence of the Cypriots, and under constant US pressure, preliminary talks took place at the NATO conference in the autumn of 1958. On 11 February 1959 a formal agreement was signed in Zurich by the Foreign Ministers of Turkey and Greece. Eight days later, the agreement was ratified in London and countersigned by the British and the Cypriots, after considerable pressure had been put on Makarios. Cyprus was to have full independence within a year.

NATO unity was thus preserved. British, Greek and Turkish diplomats rejoiced over the triumph of goodwill and international understanding. But reality proved to be more complicated. The new republic had been given a completely unworkable constitution, based on an impossible mixture of Greek and Turkish attitudes. On paper it was incomprehensible. In application, it was a legal monster. Instead of encouraging trends to integration, it made the separation of the two communities into an institution. The (necessarily) Greek President could be vetoed by the (necessarily) Turkish Vice-President on almost any essential day-to-day decision. The Greeks were to have 70 per cent and the Turks 30 per cent of all governmental, administrative and state positions, except for the Army, where the ratio was to be 60 to 40 per cent. For the larger towns, the constitution required separate municipalities, both administratively and geographically. Taxes were to be collected on a community basis. This was not a case of guaranteeing minority rights. Cyprus was given two governments – a majority one and a minority one – functioning together and overlapping. As Charles Foley has pointed out

(*Legacy of Strife*, p. 164), Cyprus was the first country in the world to be denied majority rule by its own constitution.

The Archbishop returned to Cyprus on 1 March 1959. Fifteen months later he became the first President of the independent Republic of Cyprus. But it was hardly possible for his administration to function normally. Despite all his efforts and those of the Turkish Vice-President, Dr Kutchuk, tension between the two communities rapidly built up once more. By 1963 the deadlock was complete, and at last Makarios decided to take a decisive step that would enable him to have an administration again. On 5 December, he announced his intention of unilaterally amending the constitution.

This caused an immediate crisis, more dangerous than ever. On Christmas Day a Turkish fleet was approaching Cyprus, and for two months bitter fighting on the island was accompanied by continual threats of Turkish military intervention. Strong US pressure and Soviet threats contributed to the avoidance of war. But bloodshed continued, and it seemed that nothing could put an end to it except the presence of a powerful neutral police force that would keep Greeks and Turks in Cyprus from one another's throats. Makarios turned to the UN. Simultaneously, however, the US – pulling strings to make the UN take its time – proposed a NATO 'solution'. A NATO mixed force would come in to separate the combatants. Security considerations would then make its permanent presence necessary, and the island would become a NATO base. Makarios's neutralist tendencies would be discouraged, and a *de facto* condominium of Greece, Turkey and NATO would perpetuate Allied military influence. Britain's over-clever use of the Turkish factor had thus produced an unexpected result: exit Britain, enter NATO – that is, the US.

Turkey and Greece were persuaded to back the scheme. The caretaker Prime Minister of Greece, Paraskevopoulos, made some objections, which were overruled after a lightning visit to Athens by the NATO chief, General Lemnitzer. Markarios, however, proved adamant. Kennedy's troubleshooter, George Ball, was despatched to Cyprus, but he could not change the Archbishop's mind. Nevertheless, the US kept up the pressure. Lemnitzer is said to have tried to impose *de facto* partition. He sent telegrams to both Greek and Turkish governments urging them to land troops on the island, which would have led to the landing of a NATO mixed force to interpose itself between Greeks and Turks and confront Makarios with a *fait accompli* (Kouloumbis, ibid., p. 184). But Makarios's determination prevailed in the end. Backed by the strong new Greek government under George Papandreou (and very unobtrusively by Britain, who now found the Archbishop too valuable to lose) he finally obtained a decision of the UN to send an expeditionary peace corps.

NATO plans had thus failed. Makarios's authority was strengthened and the UN force permitted him a margin of freedom. The crisis did not, however, subside. In August 1964 a Greek–Turkish war was imminent and was prevented at the last moment, after the Turkish air force bombed Greek–Cypriot positions in retaliation for a Grivas initiative of terrorism against a Turkish village. Once more it was a stalemate. The war had been avoided, but NATO unity was again at stake. Papandreou refused any compromise that excluded the possibility of ENOSIS, while the Turks were adamant in rejecting this. The Greek Premier consequently refused even to discuss the question in bilateral talks with Turkey. Making a common front with Makarios, he insisted that the solution should be decided by the UN. Turkey's importance in the strategic balance is far greater than that of Greece. (Turkey has an army three times as big and a much more powerful navy and air force than Greece. She is also the frontier of NATO betwen the Soviet Union and the Arab world.) Thus all NATO considerations would lead to a solution advantageous to Turkey rather than to Greece. Papandreou's position seemed to make a mutually satisfactory solution impossible. What was more important for the USA: instead of bringing Cyprus into NATO, developments in general and Greek policies in particular indicated a likelihood that Greece would eventually pull out of it. With the UN increasingly sympathetic to the Cypriot cause, a new crisis might emerge from a pro-Greek UN resolution and oblige Papandreou, who was under constant pressure from the Left, to risk a neutralist or Gaullist change of direction.

The government's fall in July 1965 was due to a complex of domestic and international factors, as we shall see below. It is significant, however, that Papandreou's successor, Stephanopoulos, immediately agreed to hold secret talks with the Turks. Papandreou's uncompromising opposition to what he called 'treason' became gradually more adamant as the domestic crisis mounted. His foreseeable victory in the next elections could not have made the NATO people very happy. It is therefore not unreasonable to speculate that the Cyprus problem was a factor which contributed to the undoubted connivance of the US military in the *coup* of 21 April 1967.

CHAPTER 12

The Rise of the Liberal Forces (1959–63)

IF the maintenance of the political stability of the Right for twelve years was to a large extent due to the repressive system analysed above, the lack of a coherent political alternative helped too. The total failure of the Plastiras government to carry out a policy of conciliation had been one of the reasons for Papagos's triumph in 1953. Once in power, Papagos managed to convey an atmosphere of authority and discipline which was undeniably welcomed after the chaos which had prevailed during the eight years since the end of the war.

The Liberals, now in opposition, were even less able than before to present an alternative of equal authority and cohesion. After the death of Plastiras they were deprived of the only leader who could claim the allegiance of the scattered constellation of political notabilities – and could capture public imagination. The large gap that had been opened between the Right and the Left thus remained to all intents and purposes unfilled by a strong Centre grouping. Many prominent Liberal personalities had abandoned the sinking ship, either by joining Papagos (like ex-Premiers Tsouderos and Kanellopoulos) or by agreeing to cooperate with him, as did George Papandreou and other so-called independents. The biggest Liberal newspaper group, owned by the Lambrakis family, also supported the Greek Rally, which could thus rely on the support of seven out of nine national daily papers. Of the many parties that had developed in opposition to Papagos, even the two most important – the Liberals under Sophocles Venizelos, and the EPEK, led by Papapolitis after Plastiras's death – inspired, if anything, open distrust. Papandreou returned to the Centre; he became leader of the Liberal Party when Venizelos retired from politics; Venizelos then changed his mind, was rebuffed by his old party, and started a new one. These events only highlighted the chaos prevailing among the Centrist forces. Successive attempts at realignment led only to new splits, mainly on the basis of personal ambitions and incompatibilities. Though there was a pressing need to set out a clear alternative policy, especially after 1954 when Papagos's social and economic measures started to show results, the Centrists could not do so.

For, while their interminable family disputes had seriously impaired their credibility, their own outlook and political line made them extremely reluctant to define a true alternative. Their differences with Papagos were only pronounced in that they were apt to conform to democratic constitutional provisions, which the Field-Marshal more or less disregarded. Beyond this, however, the Centre still represented the conservative-liberal trends of the old Venizelist tradition. Except for a small fraction of social-democratic elements, who had survived the civil war and its sequel but who were politically and ideologically crushed between Liberalism and Communism, the great bulk of the Centrists scarcely differed from the Right on the main issues of policy. Demagogic considerations often led them to criticize various aspects of the Papagos administration. Scandals were exposed and corruption was condemned in the most poignant terms. But, on the whole, criticism was confined to matters of secondary importance and the system was not attacked as such. Like Plastiras before them, but without the General's genuine love for the people, which had often led him to espouse the cause of the underprivileged beyond any ideological and programmatic conceptions, Papandreou, Venizelos, Papapolitis and Baltatzis (to name but a few of the Centrist leaders) were part of and represented the ruling bourgeoisie.

Many of the most prominent Liberal personalities had personal or family relations with the circles of big capital. They too functioned on the basis of patronage and were anxious to meet their clients' needs. Thus their dependence on the state apparatus was scarcely less pronounced than that of the government's deputies. They were, on the whole, financed by the same sources[1] and were permeated by the same fundamental preoccupation with re-election. Thus, since the question of the monarchy had been settled, there were very few differences between the Right and the Centre. They both represented the ruling bourgeoisie and had in mind the same or similar solutions for the main problems of the country. Their historical differences had by now almost evaporated. It was only the effective exercise of power that kept them apart. But the Right still had a significant advantage over the Centre: cohesion, authority and an undisputed leader who was fully supported by the US.

When, in September 1955, Field-Marshal Papagos died, finding a successor was a great problem. Markezinis, who had been the most prominent man in the Papagos government and the planner of his economic policy, had been forced to resign some months earlier after a personal dispute with his chief. (He has since re-emerged as an allegedly powerful *éminence grise* behind the colonels, after thirteen years in political limbo.) The two party Deputy Leaders, Kanellopoulos and Stephanopoulos, of whom the latter had become acting Premier during the Field-Marshal's illness, were both considered too weak to ensure the Right's cohesion. The King thereupon appointed Constantine Karamanlis as Prime Minister. He was a relatively unknown politician who had managed, through an efficiently run public relations office, to make a name for himself as an energetic Minister of Public Works. It seems beyond reasonable doubt, as we have seen, that strong US pressure contributed to this unexpected choice, which obviously went beyond the King's Constitu-

1. The financing of Greek political parties has always been secret, there being no legal obligation to publish accounts or to disclose financial sources. It is well known, however, that both parties and individual politicians were lavishly financed, especially during the electoral campaigns, by bankers, industrialists and shipowners who disbursed large sums of money in all directions including, sometimes, the Left. If this 'financing' was not always followed by the undertaking of specific obligations on the part of politicians towards the 'patrons', it contributed to the social and economic integration of practically the whole of the Greek political personnel in the world of vested interests.

tional rights. In fact, two months later American economic aid was doubled. Both Stefanopoulos and Kanellopoulos, over whose head Karamanlis had been catapulted, left the party. (Stefanopoulos joined the Liberals and eventually became the puppet Prime Minister in 1965, when the King dismissed Papandreou, while Kanellopoulos later rejoined Karamanlis as his Vice-Premier.) Apart from this, however, the Palace met with complete success. The departure of the two aspirants to the leadership was not followed by any split in the Right, who unquestioningly followed the King's choice. The Greek Rally was renamed by Karamanlis as the National Radical Union (ERE) and in the ensuing elections (1956) stood as united as ever. On the other hand, the coalition that was formed by the right-wing dissidents, the Centre and the Left, with the sole object of winning the elections, lacked the slightest ideological or functional unity. The working of the electoral system helped Karamanlis to remain in power and, naturally, the opposition coalition dissolved immediately after the elections.

The Centrists had, however, not learned their lesson yet. They suffered one more crushing defeat in the 1958 elections, when the left-wing party, EDA, came second with 25 per cent of the popular vote and seventy-eight deputies, thus becoming the official opposition. The electoral system, which favoured the larger parties and penalized coalitions, had largely contributed to increasing the Left's parliamentary representation. But the main reason for the collapse of the Centre should be found in the fact that large masses of Liberal supporters were sick and tired of the endless disputes between the Centrist leaders.

EDA was a subterfuge for the banned Communist Party and was in fact led by representatives of the exiled Communist leadership. Its hard-core followers, who did not exceed 10 per cent of the population, came mainly from the workers and the remnants of the leftist intelligensia. But, if few people shared the barely concealed Communist sympathies of EDA, its clear-cut ideology and programme were a model of the qualities which the Centre glaringly lacked. And its appeal was strengthened by the fact that it was unique in consistently denouncing the growing inequalities of wealth and in demanding social justice. However, the big 1958 swing to the Left did not mean a definite change in political thinking, as was soon to be proved when the Centre won back most of its lost votes as soon as it achieved some coherence and emerged as a united party again. A big section of the Liberal electorate had made a protest, more than anything else, against the fragmentation and incompetence of the Centre parties and the consequent lack of a political alternative.

But there were considerable repercussions from the unexpected replacement of the Centre by the Left as the main opposition party in Parliament. In the first place, this meant the partial dismantling of the ghetto in which the Left had been imprisoned since the end of the civil war. Now that it had almost a third of the seats in Parliament, its voice could no longer be silenced. What was more important was that, regardless of the circumstances which had led to the Left's comeback, both the Right and the USA were seriously anxious. If the trend were to continue, Greece would see a political polarization which might prove very difficult to accommodate within the parliamentary system.

The Right met the challenge by reviving the intermittent war which it had been waging against the Left since it came to power. Adding to his arsenal the threat presented by EDA's new strength, Karamanlis intensified his system of coercion. It is significant that the 'parallel state' was perfected only after the 1958 election, almost ten years from the end of the civil war and when the Right had been in power for six years. The results were to be felt in the next election, three years later.

The defeat of 1958 was the most severe suffered by the Liberals since 1920. Seeing that they had no hope of returning to power without a radical reorganization, the Centre leaders had to come to terms with one another at last. Yet it took them another two and a half years to overcome the difficulties, and it was only in September 1961, in face of impending new elections, that the Centre Union was formed as a united party. Then, eight years after losing power, practically all the political forces placed between ERE and the Left managed to regroup themselves in one political unit, jointly led by George Papandreou and Sophocles Venizelos.

US influence seems to have played an important part in this. The Americans still supported Karamanlis; but they considered, especially after the re-emergence of a powerful Left, that a strong Centre party was needed so that they could preserve their influence in a political world that would be bi-partisan, conservative and pro-American. So they systematically urged the Liberals to get together, and even implied that they would eventually welcome a Centre government.

The creation of the Centre Union was a major political event. For the first time since the war, there was an alternative to the preponderance of the Right. The election of 29 October 1961 was therefore of great importance. Despite the extremely oppressive atmosphere in which it was held, the Centre Union got 33.5 per cent of the votes. At first sight, ERE had succeeded in strengthening its position. But the line-up which had now emerged – of three distinct blocks, Right, Centre and Left – could only lead sooner or later to its fall.

The Americans were satisfied. US Ambassador Briggs declared: 'The elections have given concrete proof of the Greek people's faith in the ideals of individual freedom and human dignity' (*Le Monde*, 29 December 1961). Now that they had got a Centre opposition, they could again openly support the Right.

However, the role of loyal opposition did not satisfy the Centre. The smell of battle had brought back the memory of past victories. On the morrow of the elections, Papandreou launched a full-scale attack on Karamanlis, challenging the results and exposing the whole oppressive system that had been used. This strengthened the unity of the party and met with widespread, and somewhat unexpected, popular support. Many voters, especially among the lower middle classes, had voted for the Right purely because they feared a return to unstable coalitions and political anarchy. But they were also increasingly scared of the extremes to which the 'parallel state' was going, and now they were more and more inclined to abandon ERE and hope for a Centre government. In addition, since the Centre Union had not only survived its electoral defeat but also attacked ERE with remarkable firmness and perseverance, a significant number of people who had temporarily turned to EDA returned to the rejuvenated Centre.

But, if the creation of the Centre Union heralded an alternative government, it did not yet define an alternative policy. At first, the new party was little more than a regroupment of the political personnel who had been kept out of power for so many long years. It had broadened its political base, but not by virtue of a clear social and economic programme corresponding to the hopes of the classes whose support it sought.

Neither the structure of the Centre Union nor its (unstated) ideological premises bridged the gap between party policy and the needs and demands of the people. George Papandreou's incredible stamina and dynamism soon pushed Venizelos into second place, especially after the launching of the 'intransigent struggle' which was inspired and led personally by Papandreou. The result was that Papandreou ran the party with a disregard for internal democracy and formal rules which worked out not very differently from the autocratic way in which Karamanlis ran ERE. Papandreou could not achieve quite the same authority over his colleagues, since his party was not in power and he had no patronage to dispense; but he did his best to subordinate them to his own charisma. Using his personal charm and his public image, he managed to impose obedience on his followers in Parliament. Since slogans were enough to win him massive support, he felt no need for a party machinery functioning on democratic principles, which would have provided a permanent basis for an interplay of ideas and policies between leaders and members, and thus for working out a clear political programme.

On the other hand, the Centre Union's relations with business – while nearly as amicable as those of ERE – were undergoing a significant change. The Centre had not lost its old link with the bourgeoisie. In so far as the country's development had produced economic tycoons or an economic oligarchy, these interests had found their natural expression through Liberal political leaders. Indeed, it was the 'big business' element that was the spearhead of economic reform in the formative period of the Liberals before the First World War; and it continued to support them during the inter-war years, even when the lower middle class became more conservative and supported the Populists. By the late fifties, however, the picture was vastly different. Whereas big business before the war had consisted mainly of tycoons returning from the diaspora of Greek settlements round the Mediterranean (hence the strong pro-British connexion), in the fifties and sixties it was dominated by several new groupings.

Fortunes had been made in the immediate post-war years by those who had benefited from Marshall Aid programmes. Public works and house-building made fortunes for contractors and land speculators alike. Finally, international tycoons who had built themselves up during the world war, the Korean war boom and the Suez crisis also took advantage of the terms for attracting foreign capital which the Right had been offering since 1953. (Niarchos, Onassis and Pappas come to mind.) Naturally, all these new interests tended to back the government party, from which they had to extract contracts and privileges. ERE, being in power until 1963, benefited more than its opponents. The Centre, especially its conservative wing under Venizelos, was on good terms with business too.[2] But good relations were one thing and common interests quite another. The long period of right-wing government inevitably produced links between the economic and political Establishments – links which left little room for sharing with others. With big investments in particular, where the size of Greece made it inevitable that virtual monopolies would operate in

2. Among the party's most prominent personalities were a beer magnate (Petros Garoufalias, whom we shall meet again), a banker, a shipowner and a tobacco exporter. Others were as notoriously corrupt as some of their ERE counterparts. Venizelos, the co-leader of the party, was a shipowner himself. He had excellent relations with the banking and industrial Establishment, besides being a close personal friend of the King.

several branches of industry, business and government had been so intimately linked through the process of granting privileged terms and concessions that they were almost indistinguishable. Once a deal was made, the vested interest which ensured its preservation became almost part of the state machine. These interests became so connected with Karamanlis and ERE that they were, on the whole, unwilling to endanger their privileged position through risking any change of government. Thus, although a significant section of the bourgeoisie supported or at least was well inclined towards the Liberals, the process of rapid and anarchic economic development had created new sets of vested interests, which were becoming more and more powerful within the nexus of the economic oligarchy and whose support for the Right was unqualified and unrestricted.

The 'intransigent struggle' was at first mainly focused on the formal characteristics of the state structure developed by the Right, which appeared to be a permanent barrier to the return of the Centre to power. The demand for democratization and the exposure of scandals, corruption and the ineffectiveness of ERE were the main pivots around which the opposition attacks were centered. Though Papandreou's personal interest in problems of education produced a programme of radical changes in the educational system, the Centre's social and economic programme did not go further than a more or less general promise of fair play, justice and reorganization. Despite their vagueness, however, the Centre's positions had a curiously sharper appeal than the detailed defences by ERE of their own achievements. 'The numbers,' said Papandreou, 'seem to be doing well. It is the people that suffer.' Nor was it only Papandreou's unrivalled ability to talk to the masses which made them captive. He had simply caught the yearning of the working people, and particularly of the peasantry, for some social justice. Whereas the government were proud to announce impressive rates of economic growth, their ideology as well as their connexions with profiteering business made them unwilling to think about income redistribution. Papandreou, by contrast, realized that rapid economic growth meant growing inequality, particularly for the masses of the agrarian poor, who started the move towards foreign emigration during this period. What were in a sense no more than slogans, such as pensions for old peasants, higher price support for their products, free medical treatment, and most persistently education for their children, thus became for the rural masses what no cool-headed political programme could ever become. For a whole year, and while sophisticated politicians doubted whether the game was a winner, the old man was trekking the countryside in a curiously enthusiastic yet almost mystical communion with the people. Thus, oddly enough, the main tenets of the Centrist campaign were developed in the process of the 'intransigeant struggle' and did not derive from a preconceived platform. They were never crystallized into a coherent system of targets and priorities. More than anything else, it was a new attitude of government towards the people that Papandreou advocated. He still remained in his heart a Liberal of the old school. If his concern with a more equitable income redistribution was undeniable, it was within the prevailing socio-economic structure that he hoped to carry out his promises.

Throughout 1962 Papandreou's attacks became increasingly fiercer. After denouncing the electoral 'farce' of 1961, Papandreou gradually started attacking every aspect of the system. The ERE government was described as a 'gang' clinging to power by illegal means, the role of the army was exposed and the royal 'service' government which had been formally in power during the electoral period was stigmatized.[3] The King was called on to dismiss Karamanlis and hold

3. Governments in power usually resigned during election periods and were replaced by 'service' governments whose impartiality guaranteed the impeccable conduct of elections. The 1961 electoral 'orgy' to use Papandreou's phrase, took place under the presidency of General Dovas, a former Army Commander-in-Chief, and military adviser to King Paul. Appointed by the King and including persons notorious for their ultra-Right opinions, the government could not claim impartiality even as a joke. The composition of the post-war service governments supposedly made out of senior civil servants is significant: 30.8 per cent of their members were university professors, 14.1 per cent members of the judiciary, 13.1 per cent

a new election. When he refused, the Palace in turn was made the object of severe attacks. The monarchy in itself was not called into question, but the activities of royal advisers were bitterly attacked and the King was told insistently to return to his proper constitutional role.

As time went on, the attacks became fiercer and fiercer and were directed against virtually all the institutions which the Right had misused and injured. By early 1963 the situation was indeed explosive. Stimulated by the Centre Union's uncompromising attitude, a series of demonstrations against the government started. All over the country, in towns and villages alike, people of every class showed their profound discontent. A wave of rallies, strikes and demonstrations shook the country. The police handled demonstrations with unyielding sternness. Mass arrests and intensified measures of repression by agents of the 'parallel state' only made grievances more bitter. When a peasant was shot dead by the gendarmerie at a big demonstration of tobacco-growers in Central Greece, dozens of rallies of angry people all over the country challenged the ERE government's right to rule.

Things came to a head in May 1963. Gregory Lambrakis, an EDA deputy, was murdered in Salonica in the presence of a large number of policemen, outside the hall where he had addressed a meeting of his party. The murder served as a catalyst for the pressure that had been gathering, as well as a symbol for the intolerable oppression. Journalists did the job of the investigating authorities who, in the beginning, showed negligence, to say the least. Gendarmerie General Vardoulakis, who was originally in charge of the investigations, was later condemned to imprisonment and dismissed because he had put pressure on witnesses to withhold material evidence. It was soon proved that the murder had been com-

---

industrialists, 12.8 per cent pensioned generals, 12.6 per cent members of liberal professions, and only 8.9 per cent senior civil servants. Under a different classification 52 per cent were members of boards of public enterprise or private businessmen, 22 per cent had been general secretaries of ministries (a purely political post), 12 per cent were members of the royal Court and 8 per cent members of the Academy of Athens.

mitted by members of an extremist right-wing organization in full collaboration with the local police. While the affair was taking on an unprecedented scale, senior police officers were gradually implicated. The local gendarmerie chief, and the gendarmerie Commander-in-Chief of Northern Greece, General Mitsou, were proven to have had full knowledge of the plot to murder Lambrakis.

Though an attempt was made to maintain a curtain of silence around the affair, a task that was undertaken by the Supreme Court Prosecutor Constantine Kollias (a King's man and Premier after 21 April 1967), the implication of the police officers could not be hidden. Kollias managed, however, to block investigations at this point. Although the police officers' role as immediate instigators of the murder was not in doubt, their exact role and position within the 'parallel state' as well as their real motives and possible connexions with higher circles of the Army, the government or the Palace were never disclosed. The Karamanlis government was, however, shaken. 'Who in God's name governs this country?' Karamanlis is reported to have shouted in exasperation when he was informed about the circumstances of Lambrakis's murder. It was not long before he knew the answer. A few weeks later and as the storm was reaching its paroxysm, Karamanlis was reported as disagreeing about a state visit the royal couple were about to make to London. On this pretext Karamanlis resigned – or was fired – and was replaced in the Premiership by another King's man, Panayiotis Pipinelis (now Papadopoulos's Minister of Foreign Affairs).

The true reasons for the dismissal of Karamanlis, who had presided over the longest uninterrupted government in Greek history, were of course different. The inside relationship between Karamanlis and the Palace and Army circles had been deteriorating since the 1961 elections, while the enmity between the Premier and Queen Frederika (the King's 'strong man') was an open secret. Nevertheless some mystery remains. His refusal to put up the slightest struggle for his position and prestige, and his sudden departure from the country under a false name (Mr Triantafyllides), gave rise to rumours that his life had been threatened. Karamanlis himself, who has lived in Paris since 1963, has never offered an explanation or even a hint. It has been implied that he had been waging a secret battle against the royal control of the 'parallel state', with the ultimate object of curtailing royal prerogatives as much as possible, and strengthening governmental authority under his own leadership. This view is corroborated by Karamanlis's persistent attempts to introduce a 'Gaullist' amendment to the Constitution, in which he was finally unsuccessful. It has been further implied that the electoral falsification of 1961 was put into effect against the will of the Premier in order to discredit him personally, and to strengthen the cohesion of the Right around the Palace, which would then be able to choose a more malleable person as Premier.

The chief reason for Karamanlis's fall is, however, to be found in the growing climate of internal strife that had resulted from the 'intransigent struggle'. Much more than the ERE government was in danger once the King was involved in the political arena. Once again, as during the civil war, it seemed that the Liberals might be the best safety valves to avoid the bursting of the system. If the party could be decapitated in the process, so much the better. Venizelos, who had very reluctantly followed Papandreou in his 'intransigent struggle', and the King, who had started to feel its consequences, were constantly seeking ways of reversing the trends which were leading towards political polarization. With both protagonists, Karamanlis and Papandreou, off the scene, vast possibilities of compromise would be opened, in which the Right would certainly be able to outmanoeuvre the few progressive elements of the Centre.

A move in this direction was attempted immediately after the Pipinellis government assumed office. Sophocles Venizelos, supported by a large fraction of the Centre Party, attempted to support the Pipinellis government in Parliament, thus practically putting an end to the 'intransigent struggle' and undermining Papandreou's authority. But the latter's reaction was fast and vigorous. Supported by large demonstrations of popular indignation, he immediately expelled

Venizelos from the party and refused to compromise. Approaching eighty, Papandreou – once the master of compromise and suavity – obviously liked his new role. His charisma had at last, after forty years of political life, made him a national popular leader. His adamant position broke Venizelos's resistance, and obliged him to retreat. The Centre Union resumed its struggle and exerted renewed pressure for immediate elections.

The King finally decided to give in. Return to political normality was the only way towards a reconciliation of the Centre and the Palace. Consequently, though Pipinellis won a vote of confidence in Parliament (a fact that shows the extent of the King's influence over the Right, whose chief he had expelled only some weeks ago) a general election was called for November. The service government appointed was a clear signal that the elections would be free: its President, Stylianos Mavromichalis, President of the Supreme Court, was a lifelong Liberal. The experienced Greek voter immediately knew that this deal between the King and the Centre signified that the Army would stay in its barracks. Without the Army's open or covert support, the Right was obviously on the defensive. In the elections that took place on 3 November, the Centre Union emerged as the leading party with 42 per cent of the votes (as against 33.6 per cent in 1961), mainly at the expense of ERE, who fell from 50.8 per cent in 1961 to 39.3 per cent. Papandreou was called on to form a government. The Right's twelve-year rule had come to an end.

CHAPTER 13

The Centre Union in Power (1963–5)

THOUGH the elections of 3 November had brought Papandreou to the Premiership, the Centre Union did not have an absolute parliamentary majority. Refusing to form a coalition government with the Right, or to depend on the support offered him by the Left, Papandreou resigned and opted for new elections which, he hoped, would give him an absolute majority. The new elections took place on 16 February 1964 and were a triumph for the Centre Union. With an unprecendented 52.72 per cent of the votes (against 35.26 per cent for ERE and 11.80 per cent for EDA), it had an ample majority in Parliament. The electoral triumph of Papandreou, whose personal position in the party had been strengthened after the death of Sophocles Venizelos (his life-long antagonist, and leader of the Royalist faction of the party), can largely be attributed to the extensive liberalization and democratization that immediately spread in the countryside during his first short government. Though the state apparatus was still completely in the hands of the Right (it is significant that in the border regions, which remained under military authority, ERE got between 62 per cent and 70 per cent of the votes), coercion had on the whole been restricted to a marginal role. It is true that the Centre victory was to a certain extent helped by EDA's decision to put up no candidates in twenty-two out of the fifty-five electoral districts, where its strength was insignificant. Its share of the vote thus fell from 14.34 per cent in 1963 to 11.80 per cent in 1964. The Right made much of this, as 'objective' proof of Papandreou's 'collaboration' with the Communists. In fact, the real strengthening of the Centre did not come from the Left but from the Right, whose share of the poll fell from 43.10 per cent (including Markenizis's tiny party) to 35.26 per cent (again including Markenizis, who collaborated with ERE this time).

The switch from Right to Centre was most spectacular in the countryside. In Athens and Salonica, which account for six electoral districts, ERE more or less maintained its vote. Crete (four electoral districts) had always voted overwhelmingly for the Centre for historical reasons and had been exempted from the system of police repression. In the other forty-five districts – covering the rural areas and small towns of Greece – ERE had an absolute majority in thirty-three in 1961, nine in 1963 and only three in 1964. The Centre Union won an absolute majority in twenty-six of these districts, compared to four in 1963 and none at all in 1961.

Hence, what worried the Right even more than the coming to power of a Centre government was this clear proof of the fragility of their machinery of coercion which had served them so efficiently for over a decade. Papandreou's declared intention to liberalize Greece in a thorough fashion increased the anxiety of the Establishment, who foresaw the release of pressures and demands that could not be appeased within the framework of the system. If three months of 'liberty' had been enough for the crumbling of an edifice that had taken twelve years to build, then the fulfilment of Papandreou's programme threatened to disrupt the electoral balance for good. The new class alliance now taking shape – between large masses of the peasants, the working class, and the radicalized middle and lower bourgeoisie – would leave the Right as a permanent and shrinking minority. There was genuine shock that so much of the old order seemed to be overthrown so quickly. So the slogan of the 'Communist menace' was raised without delay. George Rallis, son of the Quisling Prime Minister, Minister of the Interior under Karamanlis, and one of the most powerful ERE politicians, said cynically: 'The roles have now been reversed. Whereas the Communists did not dare to state their opinions, it is now the nationalists who have to disguise their convictions. George Papandreou is probably not a man belonging to the extreme Left. But *the heavy blow he has dealt to anti-Communism entitles us to regard him as the Kremlin's agent in Greece*' (quoted by Eric Rouleau in *Le Monde*, 11 September 1965).

Immediately after the Centre Union took power, the Right did its utmost to discredit the new government. The assault started on the economic front. Allegedly because of Papandreou's policy of increasing agricultural subsidies, wages and pensions, an unparalleled attack was launched by ERE on the currency. Papandreou was accused of endangering the stability of the drachma, and the public were told that the only safeguard for the value of their savings was to hoard gold. In response to this campaign, deposits were withdrawn from the banks and gold sovereigns were purchased in the open market, where the price of gold soon soared. The authorities felt obliged to sell gold, thus depleting the official reserves. Suggestions to freeze the gold market were rejected from fear of creating more panic.

The attack cut sharply. One of the undeniable achievements of the Right, and the cornerstone of their financial policy, had been the maintenance of a remarkable price stability. The decade between 1953 and 1963 was probably the only period Greeks could remember when the country was not haunted by inflation. But the government held firm and the momentary panic, apparently started through the withdrawal of some large depositors' funds, was not followed by bigger withdrawals. After two months the fever subsided, the Central Bank started repurchasing its gold, the money returned to the banks, and the drachma remained stable. Despite some reiterated prophecies of impending disaster, price stability remained for the duration of the Papandreou government. Eventually, after some inflation had resulted from the handouts distributed by the puppet governments which followed Papandreou's dismissal, the gold market was closed.

The Centre Union continued the ERE economic policy with respect to the industrial infrastructure. But in other fields it made big changes. A major effort was made to redistribute income: agricultural subsidies and support prices were increased, minimum wages rose, and the result was a considerable rise in the incomes of both peasants and workers. The consequent increase in consumption mopped up all excess capacity in local manufacture, and a healthy industrial boom soon replaced the chronic stagnation of the industrial sector. The fact was that the Right had been too conservative in its monetary policy. Though it had provided the economy with a considerable modern infrastructure, private investment had remained stuck in housing or simply in land speculation, to the detriment of manufacture in particular. By contrast, the Centre was thoroughly Keynesian. Income redistribution was seen as a tool of effective demand stimulating domestic consumption. And indeed expansion was very rapid. In 1965, for the first time, the value of industrial output surpassed that of agricultural production.

In another sector, too, the Centre's economic policy broke with that of ERE. Different ideas about foreign investment prevailed. After difficult negotiations, the terms agreed by ERE regarding the two biggest foreign ventures – the Pechiney aluminium development and the Esso-Pappas chemical complex – were revised and new terms, more advantageous for Greece, were imposed.

On the whole, the economic policy pursued in the first period of the Centre Union government did not alienate the Greek bourgeoisie. Business was good and profits were high. The system of fiscal and tariff privileges was maintained, the credit system was eased, the rate of economic expansion went up to about 8 per cent in real terms, and prices were kept steady.

On the other hand, Papandreou's policy towards the 'parallel' structure of power became extremely suspect in the eyes of the Right. Within a few months, a climate of freedom had been almost completely restored. Coercion by the police and gendarmerie virtually disappeared, a number of extremist right-wing bands were dissolved, the majority (but not all) of the political prisoners were released, and the 'certificate of national probity', though officially maintained, fell into disuse. The results of the liberalization were enormous. Political democracy was at last functioning again, for the first time since 1935 a full thirty years since the Right had taken over. An unprecedented ferment of ideas, debates, political and cultural activities created a totally new climate. Among students, professionals, workers and peasants alike, a universal eagerness to join in working out new schemes and solutions to problems almost shook the foundations of society. The lethargic backwaters of an underdeveloped country suddenly became a lively social experiment. A completely reformed educational programme which was put forward by the government constituted, for all its shortcomings and contradictions, a great step forward which stirred up the swampy waters of Greek education. The creation of a third University in Patras, and the plan for the establishment of two others in Crete and Epirus, gave a great impetus to the antiquated cultural and educational scene. Compulsory schooling was extended from six to nine years and free school meals in all primary schools in the countryside (partly supplemented with limited scholarships for secondary schools) made the law's provisions realistic in a country where poor parents would rather use their children's labour. Of all Papandreou's reforms, by far the most popular was the chance seen by the peasants for their children to become 'civilized human beings'. (Free school meals and the extension of the leaving age were both abolished by the colonels directly after the 1967 *coup*.)

Papandreou also tried to establish a free trade union movement by changing the structure of the General Confederation of Labour. He promulgated a law making representation proportional to the numbers of actual membership. The effect would be to liberate the unions from twenty years of control from above. Though the US-dominated ICFTU (International Confederation of Free Trade Unions) intervened and managed to modify the reform, a degree of genuine representation was achieved for the first time.

The thorough change in the political atmosphere quickly stimulated a radical mood among both peasants and workers. A widespread movement of wage claims and demands soon got going, and although the government was not openly challenged – at least, to begin with – many strikes and demonstrations took place. The government's attitude was much more liberal than that of its predecessor, but a number of serious clashes between demonstrators and police were not avoided. From the summer of 1964, pressure from the underprivileged classes mounted steadily. The Left naturally took as big a part as they could, on both ideological and tactical grounds. Their problem was how to stop the erosion of EDA in favour of Papandreou, whose policies were obviously popular and who was remedying at least some of the grievances which had kept the Left united for so long. This intensified the fears of the Right, as it was becoming more and more obvious that the Centre Union would be gradually pushed by pressure from below. Under the leadership of the Prime Minister's son Andreas, an economist who had been a professor in the USA, a powerful left wing developed within the Centre Union, pressing for more vigorous reforms. The struggle within the party for a determined reform policy was still in its early stages. But it was quite clear to the Right that the mounting pressure of social demands, released by political liberalization, could only lead sooner or later to the Centre Union adopting a radical policy.

The personal ambitions of many Centre Union politicians, who had hoped to succeed the ageing Prime Minister, converged with the Establishment's growing suspicions of the newly defined role of Andreas Papandreou. Threats that the party would split if Andreas were not discouraged eventually had an effect on the Prime Minister. After Andreas was found to be involved in a transaction concerning the assignment of a large research project to a personal friend, an all-out attack by the Right and some of his colleagues compelled him to resign from his post of Deputy Minister for Co-ordination. It was the first time since the war that a Minister had resigned because of being implicated in a 'scandal', in a country where it was common knowledge that many politicians were involved in extremely shady transactions. Probably for this reason, Andreas Papandreou's prestige scarcely suffered from the incident. In later events, his dismissal did him more good than harm.

However, the government did not push hard at vital points. It stood firm in dealing with the epiphenomena of the police state, but did not attack its foundations except rhetorically. Despite changes in the senior personnel of the police, despite the atmosphere of freedom, despite the liberalization in the trade unions, the most important weapon of the Right – the Army, stronghold and last resort of the system of vested interests – was not touched at all. Thus, while the apparatus of oppression was prevented from functioning, and while this caused grave concern to the Establishment who had built it up, the structure itself remained intact.

It was for fear of pushing the Palace too much that Papandreou committed his fatal mistake. Not only did he abstain from interfering with the Army's structure, which in opposition he had so relentlessly exposed; he even appointed as Defence Minister Petros Garoufalias, the beer magnate and the King's favourite, who, alone in his party, had refused to take part in the 'intransigent struggle' which overthrew Karamanlis. It seems that the appointment of this obvious fifth columnist to the most crucial, in view of the circumstances, governmental post was not even demanded by the King but was 'offered' by Papandreou as a gesture of good will. Papandreou obviously had not forgotten King Paul's address to the armed forces that had created a great uproar among the political world. 'I belong to you and you belong to me,' he had said. From what followed, it is obvious that it was not a 'façon de parler'.

The same concern for not pushing things too far was manifested in all activities of Papandreou in relation to what could then be considered as the royal domain. The royal allowance was almost doubled, the Queen-Mother Frederika (whose allegedly nefarious influence on royal 'politics' had given rise to a widespread demand to cut short her privileges) was protected by the promulgating of a special decree forbidding all criticism of her person, and was offered a pension of $100,000 a year. King Paul had died on 6 March 1964 and been succeeded by his son, Constantine II. Partly because he thought he could outmanoeuvre the young King, partly because he was under pressure from those right-wing elements in his party who were provoked by Andreas's bid for the succession, George Papandreou's line was to flatter the King rather than to curtail his powers.

Thus, while the Premier was hesitating and vacillating, caught in the eternal Liberal dilemma of whether to worry more about the challenge from the Left or the pressure from the Right, his position was being slowly and steadily undermined. His increasingly independent foreign policy, shown in the Cyprus impasse, was arousing second thoughts among US officials, who found him less malleable than they had expected. Though his loyalty to NATO and the Western alliance was unchanged, it was clear that the Centre could not be trusted to obey orders unquestioningly as ERE had in the past. Papandreou's refusal to accept the NATO solution for Cyprus was not his only sign of independence. He took measures to end the total dependence of the Greek secret services on the CIA. He refused to allow the Greek Army to take part in the NATO military training exercises in August 1964. He could not or would not prevent the pro-government press from showing a strongly anti-American spirit. He sat back while Makarios accepted Communist weapons. Finally, despite strong NATO pressure, he planned to reduce military expenditure.[1]

American displeasure with political developments was increased by the fact that the growing consciousness of class interests, in quarters that had formerly been docile, threatened not only to destroy the electoral balance, but also to colour class antagonisms with a strong anti-American and neutralist tinge. The political crisis that had led to the fall of Karamanlis had been solved only too well. Contrary to the hopes of the Establishment, the new government achieved political stability. But in reality the crisis was deepening. The sharp movement for social and economic demands was steadily entrenching itself in the left wing of the Centre Union, under the leadership of Andreas Papandreou.

His meteoric rise is not unconnected with the growth of a broad group of technocrats, intellectuals and administrators;

1. The Army's reaction is best illustrated by the astonishing statement of General Frontistis, formerly Chief of Staff and since 1959 an ERE deputy. 'Is the Government prepared to take this step?' he asked. '*Will it find a military leadership that will accept it?*'

their ideological inclination towards a new rationality and efficiency made the technocratic economist, who had developed a Kennedy-style reputation for straight talking, an attractive figure for them. Having espoused the cause of radical change, he managed to capture the imagination of vast 'newly liberated' audiences in both city and countryside.

The main social force behind Andreas was the mass of underprivileged workers, petty bourgeois and peasants. Having moved far into politics during the 'intransigent struggle', they now demanded a direct hand in the political game to achieve their economic, social and cultural aspirations. For the first time in years, a non-Communist political group managed to give them hopes of radical change. And since this group was actually in the government and looked like being able to turn these hopes into reality, it was quite different from the marginal and utopian social-democratic efforts of the past. Large masses of Greeks suddenly believed that they had found a leader who was not just slightly better than the others. It was the first sign that the 'clientèle' type of political representation could be done away with.

A number of intellectuals who wanted a radical policy were concerned at the appearance of a new charismatic leader riding a wave of popular feeling. It might, they thought, hinder the development of a modern party structure, which in their eyes was needed to put the policies they advocated into effect. On the other hand, the Right went in fear of the 'many-headed monster' which they thought they had killed, and could not see the objective factors which explained the emergence of both the movement and its leader. They concentrated their attacks on Andreas's personal integrity, his ambitions, his irresponsibility. In hindsight, of course, it is easy to see the many weaknesses of the radical movement and the serious mistakes committed. It remains true, however, that the movement put down deep roots and that it truly represented the realignment of social forces after the fall of the Right. It was this new element in Greek politics that contributed to George Papandreou's gradual loss of control over his most important lieutenants, Mitsotakis, Tsirimokos, Stephanopoulos and Mavros (and, with them, the two biggest newspapers, controlled by Kokkas and Lambrakis). Thus, when he had later to fight the Palace, his party lacked both the cohesion that would have enabled him to stand his ground, and the self-confidence that had resulted from the overwhelming electoral victory.

Thus, through 1964, the Centre Union Government was being gradually obliged, by both foreign and domestic pressures, to take measures which produced growing fear among the Establishment and US officials. The Cyprus imbroglio had led Papandreou to accept an invitation to visit Moscow in the beginning of 1965. This was the beginning of the crisis that was to lead to his fall. Fearing, or more probably under the pretext of fearing, an eventual shift in Greek foreign policy towards more independence and perhaps neutralism, the US and the Right reacted with unexpected violence. Kannelopoulos, who had succeeded Karamanlis in the leadership of ERE, demanded the removal of Papandreou by his own lieutenants and obliquely promised parliamentary support if such a move were carried out. The US also pressed, mainly through the King, for the cancellation of the Moscow visit. Although popular reaction to ERE's public proposal and US intervention was widespread, Papandreou's moderation avoided an explosion with the Palace. But the trip to Moscow was adjourned *sine die*.

It was, however, only a temporary postponement of the open confrontation. Andreas's return to the government in April 1965, after extensive tours of the countryside where he had been acclaimed as the next Prime Minister, made him in effect his father's deputy. The suspicions aroused by his mildly anti-NATO stand during the Cyprus crisis of the previous summer were now intensified. The Prime Minister refused to give in to extremely strong pressure applied by President Johnson when, in the beginning of June, the Papandreous visited Washington. The failure of the 'little summit' to solve the renewed Cyprus crisis precipitated events. A number of senior CIA agents swarmed into Athens with the object of undermining Papandreou's parliamentary majority. Secret meetings between US agents and members of the government (and future defectors) were exposed; important members of the government were prepared to oust the Papandreous and accept parliamentary support from the Right. (For a detailed account see Rousseas, pp. 28–32.) Papandreou retaliated to all these attacks with the exposure of the 'Pericles' plan, a document in which the role of the Army in the electoral manipulation of 1961 was brought to light. The document had been negligently left behind by the ERE government, but Papandreou had not produced it before. The Premier stated categorically that he had decided to purge the Army of conspirators who up to that point had not been touched in the least. But this was the drop that overflowed the bucket. Papandreou had been transformed from a potentially dangerous opponent of the system into a direct threat to its major power reserve. Undermining his policy was no longer enough. He had to be eliminated before his intervention in the Army became effective.

The pretext was promptly fabricated. It was the ASPIDA case – an alleged conspiracy within the Army to overthrow the Constitution and set up a Nasserite dictatorship, implicating twenty-eight officers and a number of politicians, among whom was Andreas Papandreou. The charge was absurd in view of the small number of men involved, who could only be powerless in the framework of a predominantly Royalist army with 10,000 officers. When the case came to trial, the lack of any serious evidence was perfectly obvious. But it served its immediate purpose well. If Andreas did have some kind of connexion with Army circles, George Papandreou's decision to reorganize the Army and bring it under civilian control could be discredited as an attempt to cover his son's 'criminal' activities.

On 9 July, the Prime Minister presented the King with a list of officers to be dismissed, together with a request for the removal of Defence Minister Garoufalias, who had persistently obstructed the Premier's policy. (Predictably, Garoufalias was appointed Prime Minister for a few hours when the

King made his pathetic attempt to get rid of the colonels on 13 December 1967.) Constantine refused to discuss the problem and left for Corfu on holiday. Garoufalias refused to resign and was expelled from the party on 13 July. Despite this, he insisted on staying in charge of his ministry. Meanwhile, frantic efforts were being made by the King's private secretary and by US officials and agents to find enough Centre Union dissidents to overthrow Papandreou 'legally'. When they thought they had arranged this 'solution', Constantine summoned Papandreou and refused to accept the nomination of a new Defence Minister or to dismiss the officers. Papandreou replied by proposing to take over the Defence Ministry himself, a solution which the King flatly rejected on the 'moral' grounds that this would impede the investigations regarding Andreas. The Premier then threatened to resign. The King hurriedly accepted this resignation, which had not been formally offered, and Papandreou found himself outmanoeuvred. Within two hours – and this shows how carefully the advance plans had been made – a new government of dissident Centre Union men was sworn in, under Athanassiades-Novas, President of the Chamber of Deputies.

The King had won the first round. Papandreou had been ousted, and Andreas was under indictment for high treason.

CHAPTER 14

King's Coup or Colonels' Coup? (1965–7)

THE ousting of George Papandreou on 15 July 1965 was only the first of a series of undisguised interventions in politics by the King. If volumes of Byzantine argument were poured out as to whether or not the King was within his formal constitutional rights, it is beyond discussion that his action openly disregarded popular sovereignty and the mandate of the voters. The problem was wrongly posed, both in Greece and abroad, when a legalistic interpretation of the provisions of the constitution was attempted. Though the King had no right, even formally, to dismiss his Prime Minister, this is beside the point. Hitherto the Crown had engaged in politics behind a smoke-screen; on 15 July all appearances were abandoned and Constantine emerged as an open maker of political decisions, in total contradiction to the democratic principles which were supposedly the foundation of the regime. A government which had taken power through an overwhelmingly popular mandate was not only systematically sapped from within, but at last simply dismissed after an elaborate piece of scene-setting.

The inadequacies and mistakes of the Papandreou government cannot be denied. But the parliamentary system, however unsatisfactory, did function to the extent that it allowed a minimum of popular control and representation in the expression of legal authority. The King's open intervention was a fatal blow at the already unstable foundations of democracy in Greece. By making the acceptability and viability of a government contingent upon the monarch's will, the principles of parliamentary democracy were abolished.

Another by-product of royal intervention was the utter cynicism and total contempt for public opinion shown in the unprecedented manoeuvres that finally led to the formation of a government of dissidents from the Centre Union. The most elementary rules of the parliamentary game were broken. In fact, there was no more game to play. The fall of Papandreou was decided on and put into effect before any political crisis was visible. It was decided to topple him – therefore, he was dismissed. The attempts to find a Centrist successor were made only to save whatever appearances could still be saved.

The defection of at least forty-five Centrist deputies was needed in order to form an alternative parliamentary majority. It took three months to assemble them, one by one, after a series of bargains unequalled in the history of the nation. The number of ministerial posts was increased until every single defector could be promised and given one, in a party which consisted exclusively of ministers. However, when a job in the puppet government was not enough to tempt prospective 'apostates' (as the defectors came to be called), large sums of money were allegedly offered on the side. There is, of course, no concrete evidence of the extent of this last resort of the royal clique, though a number of non-dissident deputies claim to have been approached. Though the extremely widespread as well as vigorous popular reaction (and probably faulty information) made the operation much more difficult than anticipated, the salami method was finally crowned with success. The third prospective Prime Minister, Stephanos Stephanopoulos, formerly Vice-Premier under Papandreou – who had solemnly declared only a few days earlier that he would never agree to form a government without Papandreou's consent – managed to achieve a parliamentary majority with the support of ERE. Though this majority was extremely weak (152 to 148), the crisis was formally solved.

The results of the formation of the new government were, however, unexpected. Contrary to the expectations of the manipulators of the crisis, the creation of an alternative Centrist government had proved far from easy. The King had defeated his own purposes, as an unforeseen element had made the plan backfire. Unprecedented in vigour and amplitude, popular indignation impeded the fulfilment of all royal intentions. For many weeks several hundreds of thousands of people daily manifested their unqualified fury against defectors and Palace alike. When Papandreou decided to drive through Athens in a ceremonial appeal to the people, the centre of the capital was filled by one million spectators and the scene was less reminiscent of a political rally than of a Roman triumph. It is not, therefore, surprising that prospective defectors should suddenly find themselves less eager to abandon a fallen chief, who now was the object of popular idolatry. When Lambrakis, owner of the largest Centrist newspaper group (unrelated to the assassinated EDA deputy), and a confirmed Centre-Right backstage manipulator, attempted to shift his position as a prelude for the abandonment of Papandreou, an angry crowd assembled around the press magnate's headquarters and huge piles of newspapers were set on fire. Lambrakis, who was making a fortune by record newspaper sales, gave in.

Thus, for the first time in years, an authentic feedback process between political activity in the broad sense and popular pressure seemed to be functioning. It was this unexpected element of direct mass participation that more than anything else endangered the royal plan. It is beyond doubt that the activity of the masses was to a significant extent due to the militant spirit of EDA and especially to the Left youth organizations, who tirelessly swarmed in the centre of Athens day after day, supporting Papandreou in his struggle. But the Left was only part of the active vanguard of a much more general and varied mass movement. The bulk of Papandreou's supporters during this period were the solid core of Centre voters. Their violent reaction was directed against the flagrant violation of democratic principles. If social connotations and anti-American (anti-NATO) feelings were in the air, the movement was not in the least subversive. It was the re-establishment and consolidation of popular sovereignty they were after, not a change of regime. But for the first time the establishment of popular sovereignty was seen by a large majority of citizens as being contingent on the permanent breaking of royal power and of the clan of vested interests.

Thus the split in the parliamentary group was not followed by a split in the Centrist electorate. Though the 'apostates' quickly organized themselves into a new party (called the FIDIK), their appeal was almost non-existent. Powerful politicians, who for many years had enjoyed great popularity both locally and nationally, suddenly found themselves devoid of any popular support. The furious attacks by the puppet government against the malpractices of the Papandreou administration were totally ineffective in the eyes of public opinion, not so much because the defectors themselves had occupied important posts in the Papandreou government, but mainly because of the despicable manoeuvres that had led to its fall, plus the fact that these attacks were seen as pretexts. Papandreou himself, on the contrary, was absolved from his sins and mistakes. No concrete criticism of his inadequacies could be effective any more in breaking his image. Whereas his contradictory administration had seriously diminished his credibility if not his popularity, his dismissal had made him into a popular hero. The 'apostates' could never hope to become anything else than what they had been in the beginning: an interim puppet government, a pawn in the royal game, a stage between Papandreou and a true Royalist government.

The King had in fact burned too many bridges. In addition to his direct involvement in the party struggle, he had endeavoured to become the ideological leader of the Right – 'Communism is a miasma born outside Greece and directed from abroad. Its ethic is lying and treachery. It corrupts and turns into an unforgivable enemy of the fatherland everyone who comes into contact with it.' This incredible statement was pronounced by the King in his New Year's address to the nation on 1 January 1966, a mere three months after his puppet government had achieved its precarious parliamentary majority and when moderation was preached by all sides.

The repercussions of the political crisis were therefore even more nefarious for the monarchy. By the fact that the majority of the big business representatives had abandoned Papandreou in the successive waves of defection, an important ideological purge had come about within the Centre Union, reviving the long-forgotten Republican tradition. Not only was the conservative element numerically weakened, but the field was left relatively open for the further advancement of Andreas Papandreou after the defection of most of the prospective successors who had been annoyed by his rise. Although the Centre Union parliamentary group was still far from anxious to adopt a more progressive policy, Andreas was the only remaining personality with any stature and appeal.

Thus, the party's orientation was affected by the coincidence of extended and radicalized popular pressure with the rise of Andreas as unrivalled Crown Prince. Even though George Papandreou tried to mollify the mounting wave of radicalism, Andreas's statements became increasingly clear in their opposition to the foundations of the socio-economic structure: 'I believe that the country's infrastructure, transport and communications, credit, and education must belong completely to the public sector.... Heavy industry should in general be public, while light industry should be private.... It is imperative that efforts should be made to reduce or even eliminate conspicuous consumption and luxury imports.... It is necessary to stop granting monopoly charters in order to attract business investment from abroad.'

It was obvious that the whole system on which the groups in power had based their profiteering was endangered. If the radical movement of which Andreas became the spokesman was by no means socialist, in the Western European sense, it most definitely intended to force the Greek ruling class into functioning within a context of modern rationality and to cut down their fiscal privileges and class advantages. The French-type economic planning he desired to put forward would canalize investments (both private and public) with some regard to longer-term social and economic objectives as well as to immediate profitability. Haphazard investment, social waste and the era of super-profits would have to end. It may be doubted whether Andreas could have actually succeeded in carrying out the programme he envisaged. A policy of rationalization would have met serious resistance, not only from the network of vested interests, but also from the middle classes, whose inclination to patterns of luxurious consumption would be difficult to reverse. Regardless, however, of the practicability of such a policy, its firm promotion had disrupted the implicit gentleman's agreement between the Right and the Centre that had been observed even during the 'intransigent' struggle of 1961–3. Panayiotis Kanellopoulos, leader of ERE, had openly stated in 1964 that 'there are no serious ideological differences between ERE and the Centre Union, the divergencies being mainly due to incompatibilities of ... attitude.' This was certainly no longer the case after the ousting of Papandreou. The key political conflict was now filled with very concrete social and economic implications. As Andreas put it: 'The Centre Union was no longer simply the party of political democracy. It was becoming the basic force for national change.'

In short, the aims of the royal intervention met with failure. The government party, FIDIK, represented nothing at all. Though the 'apostates' stayed in power for over a year, and pursued a policy of unrestrained demagogy to establish some kind of popular basis, the political polarization was so acute that they could look forward to winning votes only at the expense of ERE, on whose support the government depended for its day-to-day existence. As the constitutional deadline for new elections approached, it became increasingly obvious that the Centre Union had not only maintained but strengthened its position. The new element of clear class antagonism that imbued the political struggle added to the difficulties of the bloc in power. Because of this factor, any further attempt to split the Centre 'from above', even if successful, could only have the same nil effects as the previous ones.

Hence, so long as a focus of resistance to the royal game remained firm around George Papandreou, he was bound to be the virtually unchallenged representative of the rising wave of popular anger. This anger cemented the class alliance which had led to the Centre's political triumph in 1964. Though Papandreou had explicitly rejected any collaboration with the Left, and was adamant in refusing to drop even a hint about the possibility of a People's Front, an effective People's Front was in fact formed from below. For increasing numbers of EDA supporters were gradually convinced, in contradiction to the official EDA line, that the Centre would carry out those structural reforms which they themselves wanted. There was, therefore, very little that could be done to break the increasingly solid class alliance. At least 65 per cent of the population were immovable in their decision to vote against the royal interventionists, and only an insignificant fraction of them could be controlled by EDA. Hence, no electoral system could possibly get the Right back to power.

Even a renewal of the terrorism in the countryside could not guarantee a repetition of the 1961 results. For the situation was by now completely different. Two years of vigorous political activity in a climate of freedom had enormously increased the potential for active or moral resistance to police oppression. Also, though the Stephanopoulos government revoked most of Papandreou's measures of democratization (for example, it officially reintroduced the ERE system of control of the trade unions), it hesitated to use the full potential of the revived 'parallel state' for fear of simply playing the game of ERE, which was in direct contradiction to its own electoral interests. It was consequently very doubtful if the Right could win the forthcoming election. The majority of the bourgeoisie, which by now had totally aligned itself with the Right, was panic-stricken. With every day that passed, the margin for further manoeuvres became narrower. Though actually holding the positions of power, the Right felt completely cornered. The parliamentary game had been played and lost.

Throughout 1966, it was stalemate. Stephanopoulos continued to preside over the puppet government, while Papandreou demanded immediate elections. Meanwhile, the rift was deepened by both domestic and international events. Two major political trials, which started toward the end of the year, had far-reaching political effects. In the trial of the murderers of the EDA deputy Lambrakis, which had been pending for over three years, the connivance of the gendarmerie and police authorities was totally proved. Though the senior gendarmerie officers, in the end, were convicted only of 'abuse of power' and not of complicity in murder, the course of the trial was such that even right-wing papers had to deplore the situation in the gendarmerie. (These men were all rehabilitated by the colonels, while the judge who had conducted the investigation was discharged and arrested.)

The even more important ASPIDA trial, in which Andreas Papandreou was accused by implication, failed still more conspicuously to hit its target. The authorities soon found themselves cornered, since no evidence whatever could be produced against any one of the defendants. On the contrary, day after day, fantastic revelations about the structure and functioning of the military secret services exposed, not the defendants, but the plot that had been concocted against them. An elaborate system of tapping ministers' telephones on behalf of the KYP (the Greek CIA) was exposed; a plot against the life of George Papandreou, which had only failed for accidental reasons, was brought to light; and two officers revealed that they had been offered large sums of money to give false evidence, in order to implicate Andreas in a Nasser-style conspiracy. For the first time, it was shown how far the secret services had penetrated into all state activities. The affair was clearly taking a bad turn. Accordingly, the court went into closed session on the pretext that important state secrets would be disclosed. But the harm had been done, and unrest did not subside. When the chief defendants were sentenced to longer prison terms than Lambrakis's murderers, the uproar reached a peak. Instead of being disgraced, the convicted officers were heroes, and their memoirs written from gaol filled the columns of newspapers and popular magazines. After having made a Jaurès out of Andreas, the manipulators had twenty-eight Dreyfuses on their hands. The flop was total.

There was only one way left open to the King to win the

fight he had started without taking the risk of losing everything. George Papandreou himself was the only potential 'fifth columnist' in the Centre Union. His defection from the radical path which the party was now taking could not, by definition, backfire. If Papandreou were willing to purge the party of its radical elements (including his son) and to accept a compromise whereby he would eventually return to power in collaboration with the Right and with the King's blessing, then the Palace would have achieved its primary aim – to keep complete control of the ultimate sources of power. But whatever Papandreou's own intentions – which are very hard to understand amid the complicated tangle of bluff, counter-bluff and double-cross between the main actors in the drama – the elderly ex-Premier could not afford to play the game freely. He himself was, to a certain extent, the prisoner of the irresistible mass movement that he was leading. He also had to face the problem of the growing authority of Andreas, who had proved that he would not hesitate, if need be, to go it alone. Despite strong US pressure, Andreas refused to take part in any move toward compromise.

At this point, through the intervention of Christos Lambrakis, the Centre-Right press magnate, a concrete plan was put forward for an escape from the dilemma. Believing that the King would never allow a radical Centre Union to return to power (rumours of an ultimate military take-over had been systematically spread since 1965), Lambrakis advocated a policy of eliminating the Centre-Left and Andreas. This would inevitably lead to weakening the electoral strength of the Centre in favour of the Left, which would consist of EDA and, hopefully, of Andreas, who might be pushed toward the Left. In this way, elections could be held which would give no party an absolute majority, thus forcing George Papandreou into coalition with the Right. Lambrakis would also be able to promote his own favourite, George Mavros, as successor to the ageing Papandreou and achieve his aim of becoming the *eminence grise* of the party. The problem that would result from the strengthening of the Left and the Centre-Left could be faced in due course.

In this connexion, a series of secret negotiations took place toward the end of the year. Whether because he really believed in the threat of a military *coup* organized by the King, or because he was scared by the radical turn that his party was taking, George Papandreou agreed to a compromise.

The main clause of the agreement was that Papandreou was to support, together with ERE, an interim non-political government designated by the King and was further to refrain from any attacks against the Palace. The involvement of the King in the political controversy would thus cease, while the joint support of a royal government by the Centre and the Right alike would alienate a large enough part of the radicalized electorate to exclude the possibility of a clear majority for the Centre. In that case (the agreement ran further) a specific obligation was undertaken by the Centrist leader to form a coalition government with ERE without calling for new elections. An electoral reform was also agreed, favouring the large parties, the Centre and ERE and penalizing the small ones, EDA, the 'dissidents' and, possibly, Andreas, in case he decided to run his own party.

But the plan became known, under mysterious circumstances, to Constantine Mitsotakis, the most powerful personality among the 'dissidents'. The success of the plan would practically wipe out the 'defectors', whose only chance lay in holding the parliamentary balance. Consequently, both George and Andreas Papandreou were warned that the agreement would be published unless withdrawn. Despite the warning, however, the elder Papandreou went ahead with the scheme. ERE withdrew its parliamentary support and the Stephanopoulos government was obliged to resign. A royal government under the Governor of the Bank of Greece, Paraskevopoulos, was sworn in (20 December) and was supported by both ERE and George Papandreou.

The prospects of the plan now depended on Andreas's reaction. Having gathered around him about forty deputies, he vigorously attacked his father. The latter threatened to expel them all from the party. But while the Right held its breath, the crisis in the party subsided as quickly as it had arisen.

Andreas decided to yield to formal party discipline and support Paraskevopoulos. But not only did he not refrain from continuing his attacks on King and oligarchy; in compensation for yielding to his father, he was promised a free hand in choosing the candidates of the party. When a document, purporting to be the secret agreement between King, ERE and George Papandreou was published in *Eleftheria* by its editor Kokkas, Misotakis's *alter ego*, on 1 January 1967, it only served to invigorate Andreas. The substance of the plan had failed. The Centre Union was as intact as ever, Andreas's position was strengthened both *vis-à-vis* his father and in public opinion, the King had not been disentangled and he was now committed to new elections. The future composition of the Centre Union parliamentary group promised to be much more radical and the impending elections, for all the elder Papandreou's hesitancy and renewed moderation, would bring the Centre back to power stronger than ever. Not unreasonably, anxiety gave way to panic. For King, Army and oligarchy it was becoming more and more obvious that the continuation of formal democracy would lead to the collapse of the edifice it had taken the Right so many years to build.

But there was no unanimity among the Right on how the situation was to be faced. It is only in hindsight that it is to a certain extent possible to clarify the contradictory trends that by the spring of 1967 were beginning to develop within the framework of the Right. A significant part of ERE under the leadership of Panayiotis Kanellopoulos seemed to be against a non-parliamentary bid for power. While they were ready to use the full potential of the 'parallel state' apparatus in order to tip the electoral balance in their favour, they were not prepared to disrupt the formal constitution order. Kanellopoulos, who was by no means sure of his party's allegiance, saw that his only chance of keeping the leadership lay in the maintenance of parliamentary democracy, even if that implied a Centre victory in the short run. But his decision-making role was really nil. He could not control his own party, which was still influenced by its sybillic former leader Karamanlis from his Paris 'exile'. Nor could he control the Army, and his influence over the King was very limited. The backing he got from the most influential right-wing newspaper group, headed by Eleni Vlachou, was inadequate for him to dominate the scene.

The exact intentions of the King are still unclear. It has been established beyond any reasonable doubt that a military action under the King himself, with the cooperation of a significant part of ERE, was being envisaged as a possible solution, and that the mechanism of such a move had been carefully prepared on the basis of the NATO plan 'Prometheus', designed to counter Communist aggression. But it is still not certain whether the *coup* had been definitely decided upon and a date fixed. What has been firmly maintained is that the question of whether and when to press the button was the main topic on the agenda of a meeting of senior Generals under the chairmanship of the King, which had been planned for 21 April 1967 – on which date, as we now know, the actual *coup* was carried out.

It also remains very unclear what the so-called '*royal coup*' would have amounted to. In February, a top-secret meeting was held in Washington, where representatives of the King and the Greek Army discussed with US officials the possibilities of an Army take-over in Greece; but no operational decision was reached. Walt Rostow, who seems to have presided over the meeting, is quoted as having closed it with the Delphic words: 'I hope you understand, gentlemen, that what we have concluded, or rather failed to conclude, makes the future course of events in Greece inevitable' (Rousseas, *The Death of a Demagogue*, p. 59).

But, if the King vacillated between an immediate *coup* and a last attempt to resolve the crisis in a constitutional way, he was none the less determined not to let the situation escape his control. C. L. Sulzberger, special correspondent of the *New York Times* and a personal friend of King Constantine, wrote: 'Constantine himself resolved months ago that he would do everything possible to prevent his country from going over the cliff; that if he felt the extreme Left was likely to change Greece's regime and policy, he would act *by any means* to save the nation from disaster' (Rousseas, p. 120). Yet it seems that the young monarch, who controlled (or thought he controlled) the Army, hesitated to take measures to avert 'disaster'. He may have still clung to the hope that Papandreou would not win an absolute majority, and that a conciliatory compromise would then be reached. After all, if the Centre Union did return to full power, he could always carry out a *coup* afterwards. Only three weeks before the *coup* of 21 April, he refused to yield to Army pressure for the immediate imposition of a dictatorship, despite the insistence of the newly appointed Chief of Staff, Spandidakis (later Vice-President of the First 'revolutionary' government). Thus, the King's objections to dictatorship were not a matter of principle. If he obviously overestimated his veto power over the Army, he did nothing to ensure his authority. Having given the green light to the preparation of a military take-over plan, he certainly failed to see the consequences of freeing the officers from their scruples. We cannot know whether his repeated assurances to George Papandreou that elections would definitely take place were wilful deception or naïve over-confidence. It is a fact that he was under constant pressure from the Army to act. The election campaign was to open on 24 April. If the King was hesitant, others were not. The *coup* was carried out on 21 April.

Heaps of journalistic information have been produced to explain the putsch by lower-grade officers who allegedly appeared out of the blue to replace the Generals who had been planning it for a long time. Though this replacement was later to have immeasurable effects in the shaping of the new regime, the actual Army take-over was in essence consistent with the royal plan. The reasoning behind the envisaged *coup* and the *coup* which happened was the same: the election had to be prevented. Moreover, what made the execution of the plan objectively possible was the prevalence of the idea that the King was ready to take over. The putsch was made in the King's name, and for the first twelve crucial hours the royal acceptance was credible enough to ensure the acceptance of the *fait accompli*. Finally, the King did sponsor the *coup*, however half-heartedly, at a time when his refusal might have led to the collapse of the colonels. According to *Der Spiegel*, which has yet to be proved wrong in its facts, it was Queen-Mother Frederika who tipped the balance of Constantine's hesitancy. 'Shut up and sign,' she is quoted as ordering him. He did both.

There is very sparse information about how the colonels' *coup* was conceived, organized and executed. But the answers to the numerous questions that arise would not greatly affect an evaluation of what happened. There is nothing unique about a military conspiracy by a few men taking advantage of conditions objectively favouring a *coup*. An analysis of what these men did after they seized power, and how they have managed to keep it, is another matter; but to investigate this we should need more information than we possess. Of paramount importance, however, is the role of foreign powers and their secret services in the conception and execution of the *coup*. Unfortunately, but for obvious reasons, information about the CIA's active role is very inadequate. It is only through bits and pieces that we can gain an insight into the real course of events. It is common knowledge that contemporary events are wrapped in greater secrecy than ever, at east in their operational details. Thus, we can deduce the key ole of the CIA only from a few scraps of evidence and from a more general, and necessarily theoretical, train of logic.

What we do know is that for many years a fundamental lichotomy has been obvious in US policy in Greece, as in other countries of immediate strategic value to the US. On he one hand, diplomatic influences have represented a more r less liberal tendency, especially since the Kennedy adninistration, and have refrained, so it seems, from open inrvention in Greek domestic affairs. On the other hand, the entagon and the CIA have followed their own independent olicies, governed by narrower military and cold-war stanards. The friction that has existed since 1947 between these vo centres of US policy in Greece gradually led to virtual ck of contact between 'official' and 'unofficial' activity. ormer Ambassador Briggs is said to have complained in a

Senate hearing that there was total incoherence of policy and lack of communication between the CIA and the US Embassy.

CIA activities in Greece were not channelled solely through CIA agents. The Greek 'State Information Agency' (KYP) was infiltrated by the CIA to the extent that even its financing was guaranteed by a direct allocation of US funds, free from any control by the Greek government. Formally, this state of affairs was changed under the Centre Union government; but it is very doubtful whether the replacement of a number of senior officers was enough to dismantle a whole complex of activities that had functioned for over ten years, with standards of allegiance other than to the lawful Greek government. The declared aim of Andreas Papandreou to uproot all foreign infiltration in the Greek secret service was a good reason for making him entirely unacceptable to the CIA. It can be no coincidence that Colonel Papadopoulos, the 'brain' behind the *coup*, and a significant number of what is now the ruling junta of Greece, were KYP men who had been working with the US secret services for many years! So it is highly unlikely that the CIA was not involved in the solution chosen for the 1967 crisis.

It is known that Richard Barnum, a key CIA agent who had played an important role in the ousting of Papandreou in July 1965, was back in Athens by the beginning of 1967. He operated through the Esso–Pappas concern, whose interests were at stake as the huge contracts signed with the puppet government were questioned by the Centre Union. Pappas himself did not make a secret of his belief that Greece 'needed' a military dictatorship. It has been further established that the Boston Pappas Foundation, run by Pappas's brother, was a conduit for CIA money destined for Greece. Characteristically, a Pappas employee, Pavlos Totomis, was entrusted with the key Ministry of Public Order after the success of the *coup*. The contracts of Esso were revised in Pappas's favour soon afterwards. Another detail might also help to shape the picture. Tom Pappas is a personal friend and the main financial backer of Spiro Agnew, Nixon's obscure vice-presidential choice, who has been openly supporting the colonels since his nomination.

Spy-agent-ology as a science would not give conclusive knowledge where it not for the fact of total logistic dependence of the Greek Army on the continuous inflow of US supplies. The integration of the Greek Army in NATO, while greatly fortifying its striking power, made it permanently dependent on the United States. It is thus highly improbable that the authors of the *coup* could have dared to bluff everybody at the same time. Considering that the reaction of the King was perhaps not certain, the colonels must have made sure that they would at least enjoy the camouflaged support of the US military authorities. It is also noteworthy that the advent of the dictatorship led to an immediate resumption of a conciliatory policy towards Turkey, designed to solve the problem of Cyprus which had been simmering uncomfortably for the US for three years. The inference may well be drawn that the US could make good use of a government so totally dependent on them that it was to American advantage to help it along.

It is of course ridiculous to maintain that the dictatorship in Greece was purely a product of US intervention. If it were possible to isolate the significant element in the abolition of democracy in Greece, there is no doubt that it is the uncompromising attitude of the circle of vested interests towards any change in the antiquated and irrational socio-economic strucures. The state within the state that has never stopped functioning since 1945 was made possible by British and subsequently US policy: but in its essence it was the offspring of a bourgeoisie that refused to give up its medieval privileges. The wave of popular indignation was bound to rise against the system some time. The Communist uprising in 1946–9 was an unsuccessful vehicle for popular demands. But anti-Communism could not function as the permanent and eternal weapon to contain any pressure for change. When the crisis finally arrived in 1964, the bourgeoisie was confronted with a fundamental dilemma. Either they could give in, or they could resist with force. The choice of the latter course was probably inevitable in view of the power structure and ideological inclinations of the Greek ruling class. When Papandreou was ousted in 15 July 1965, it was already the beginning of the end. Twenty-one months later, the process had reached its logical conclusion.